GET IT TOGETHER

PUJA BHOLA RIOS

GET IT TOGETHER

A WINNING FORMULA FOR SUCCESS FROM
THE BOSS YOU NEED

Forbes | Books

Published by Forbes Books, Charleston, South Carolina.
Member of Advantage Media.

Forbes Books is a registered trademark, and the Forbes Books colophon is a trademark of Forbes Media, LLC.

Printed in the United States of America.

10 9 8 7 6 5 4 3 2 1

ISBN: 979-8-88750-114-7 (Hardcover)
ISBN: 979-8-88750-115-4 (eBook)

LCCN: 2023904055

Cover design by David Taylor.
Layout design by Analisa Smith.

This custom publication is intended to provide accurate information and the opinions of the author in regard to the subject matter covered. It is sold with the understanding that the publisher, Forbes Books, is not engaged in rendering legal, financial, or professional services of any kind. If legal advice or other expert assistance is required, the reader is advised to seek the services of a competent professional.

Since 1917, Forbes has remained steadfast in its mission to serve as the defining voice of entrepreneurial capitalism. Forbes Books, launched in 2016 through a partnership with Advantage Media, furthers that aim by helping business and thought leaders bring their stories, passion, and knowledge to the forefront in custom books. Opinions expressed by Forbes Books authors are their own. To be considered for publication, please visit **books.Forbes.com**.

To Mom and Dad, my sister, Priya, and my incredible husband, Edwin.
You always made sure I had it together.

CONTENTS

GET IT
TOGETHER

INTRODUCTION

In times of stress, before a big presentation, or in the face of setbacks, have you ever whispered to yourself, "Come on, get it together"? I'm the leader who teaches those around me how to keep all their plates spinning in the air, be fierce in all they do, reach the pinnacle of success with tangible results, and not just get it together but also *keep* it together and then grow more. I am the boss they need—the boss you need. And in these pages, I'm going to walk you through real change.

As a first-generation American from a proud, educated, driven Indian family, I was born to work hard. Most children of immigrant families will tell you hard work, education, ambition, and the duality of the beautiful yet heavy weight of our families' expectations have created us—for good or bad—in the image of those who achieve.

From the time I started my first entrepreneurial business at age thirteen, I was hardwired to get it together, keep it together, and succeed. I don't know if I ever thought there was any other option!

Throughout my entire career and finally as a C-level revenue executive of a Fortune 500 company and business coach, I've taken the lessons I absorbed and combined them with the extraordinary upbringing I had as well as my innate instincts—and I have created a real formula for success. I've seen what works. I've also watched the mistakes of leaders who are unable to get the results they want with their teams. And now in this book, I am spelling out what it takes and encouraging you with all I have. (I promise you that I will be your biggest supporter in this book. But you'll get a dose of tough love too.)

I've used my absolute passion for numbers and data to create a unique and powerful way to approach corporate and career goals as well as personal goals. I teach both individual people and teams to have a growth mindset, record revenue, and record income. Data isn't something to look at glassy eyed on an Excel spreadsheet.

Data can whisper the answers to your problems if you know how to listen.

Data can whisper the answers to your problems if you know how to listen. While numbers are fun for me, they are also a powerful tool. Yet tools are only as good as the *people* wielding them.

Over my career, which has taken me from using my own transformative leadership concepts to achieving results and success with my teams and on to the C-suite, I discovered that unlike many people who live in the world of data and produce quantifiable results, I had a true gift when it came to managing people. Over and over again, no matter what the issue was with the teams I led, we rose together and became superstars. Results have spoken the truth of what I do time and again.

A big part of my leadership has always been coaching. How could I help the people around me clarify their goals, come up with actionable steps to make them happen, *get it together*, and transform their lives and careers?

Just as I meet with my teams and my clients, so I'd love to sit down opposite you and help you define and plan your goals. However, there is just one of me and *many, many* of you, so I did the next best thing—I wrote this book.

Every chapter will cover one of the principles I use with my own clients. We will cover the following:

- Being hardwired to work hard

- Clarity about your goals

- Formulating a real plan to get there

- Relentless execution

- "Roar of the Beast" mode

- Critical thinking skills: making time to think (and why that's so important)

- My winning formula for data analytics (trust me, I am the data whisperer)

- How to spot trends

- How to strategize

- Working through the pain

- Big results—celebrate your wins!

Unlike typical business and coaching books, however, at the end of every chapter, you—my readers—and I (the boss you secretly need!) are going to have a sit-down. Straight Talk from Puja is what you need to hear the good, the bad, and the ugly. Then you will answer questions to help you strategically create your own winning formula. Don't skip that part—the results will be worth it.

It's time to learn how to get into beast mode and reach the goals you once only dreamed of.

CHAPTER 1

On Your Mark: Developing the "Get It Together" (GIT) Mindset

It's not about money or connections—it's the willingness to outwork and outlearn everyone.

—*Mark Cuban*

When I was five, my mother, like many parents, had me take piano lessons. She used to sit in the kitchen, put the timer on the stove, and sat there doing her own work or cooking while I practiced for an hour. Unlike many parents, she did not let me quit when I was bored of scales. I learned to stick with the hard (or, in today's parlance, embrace the suck) until it was part of me.

When I was a child, I never thought that *not* working hard was an option. Of course, now as an adult and as a leader, I can look around and spot the superstars. (And we'll get into that later in the chapter.) I can also spot the people not putting the work in.

But growing up, I didn't understand that I was learning through osmosis, through example, through the community I grew up in, through my parents and what they valued, and through my own force of personality and drive in knowing that perseverance will always get you ahead. By the time I embarked on my career—where I rose at lightning speed—I began to realize that my hardwired commitment to results wasn't common.

What subsequently happened was, by the time I was thirteen, I started *teaching* piano. All that hard work and diligent practice of scales and minuets led to my first job (self-employed as a young entrepreneur, no less). I had seven young students. My mother would drive me to all their houses every single week. One of the things that helped me teach my students was a weekly practice sheet I created for parents to fill out. My dad, who worked as an executive at Xerox, happily ran off copies of the sheets for me.

The practice sheet had the days of the week and a space to write in how long the child practiced, confirmed by the parent with a signature. Arriving at a lesson once, I looked at my student's sheet, and there was nothing on it. I said, "Well, I guess we just won't have a lesson this week. There's not much I can teach you if you didn't practice what we went over last week." And at that I ended the lesson.

Upset, my student's mother called my mother. The queen of hard work was unruffled and completely backed up my procedure. In the end the parent allowed her daughter to suffer the consequence of missing a lesson, and my student then understood I was serious. Now motivated, she became one of my stars at the recital in the spring.

The DNA of Grit

According to an article published in *Current Topics in Behavioral Neurosciences,* "[M]otivated behaviors involve biological and psychological processes that have undergone evolution at numerous levels, from individual molecules all the way to species-specific social organization."[1] In other words some of us are hardwired to work hard. And we're also influenced by how we are raised and the environments we are in.

I was raised around other Indian families in Canada and the United States by two parents who were each driven and educated in their own right. We all know the stories of industrious immigrants, success stories of arriving in a new country with a few dollars in their pockets and then making it or paving the way for their children to make it. Many have the same themes of education, dedication, overcoming obstacles, and hard work. Yet despite these shared themes and values, each person's and family's story is unique. What we take from it and learn from it is unique too.

When my father was sixteen, he left India to study in London. He worked during the day and studied at night and, in seven years, got both his bachelor's and master's degrees in engineering. Then he returned to India to an arranged marriage with my mother. Like something out of a novel, ten days after the wedding, they left for Canada with just a few dollars in their pockets.

My father worked for McDonnell Douglas and then Xerox. He always told me never to go into manufacturing but to go into sales. And I listened. Sales and numbers ended up being where I excelled.

---

1   Eleanor H. Simpson and Peter D. Balsam, "The Behavioral Neuroscience of Motivation: An Overview of Concepts, Measures, and Translational Applications," *Current Topics in Behavioral Neurosciences* 27 (2016): 1–12, https://doi.org/10.1007/7854_2015_402.

He was eventually transferred to Rochester, where my brainy sister and I dutifully went to Hindi school every Sunday. My father began teaching me about finances and the stock market when I was thirteen.

My mother, meanwhile, was the ultimate hard worker and multi-tasker. My sister and I have no idea how she did it. She had a bachelor's in teaching from India, but in Rochester she had to start all over, like so many people with professional backgrounds who immigrate to the United States. My father was traveling extensively, and she worked as a teacher's assistant while pursuing a master's so she could get her new degree and certification and finally teach in America. She did all that while still driving me to my students' homes for piano lessons and to my swimming practices. My sister also had her activities. Yet we never ate fast food. She ensured we had delicious homemade meals. She performed miracles—a magical blend of hard work and determination, a magic we can all access.

Like many children of immigrants, I also had a lot of responsibility. I shoveled snow in the long, snowy Rochester winters, and I trimmed hedges and mowed the lawn in the hot, mosquito-infested summers.

In the Indian community we were part of, there was this expectation (which I defied) to accomplish this or that so my parents could have bragging rights. Culturally parents aspired to proclaim, "Oh, my child is a doctor [or lawyer or some other professional job]." My mom always said, from the time I was sixteen till I was forty, that I was extraordinarily rebellious. She's kidding (sort of), but that desire to forge my own path has resulted in my own magic blend of outside-the-box thinking with a hardwired work ethic.

Motivational Leadership for Hard Work and Success

As my career started to climb, I noticed that my teams always defied expectations. In the process of writing this book, I realized I learned certain things over my entire life, starting at a young age.

My father led my whole family in learning the lessons of hard work as an immigrant and a first-generation American. He was an extraordinary leader. He used to bring my sister and me into his offices, and people would just flock to him. And then when my family (without me—I remained to attend college) moved to China, my father ran the whole plant there. I would go, of course, during holiday time. I watched the way people reacted to him as he walked the factory floor. It wasn't because he was their boss; it was because they cared about each other. He knew about their families, he knew about their kids and that their elderly parents were staying with them, he knew about what was going on in their lives. The amount of information he had about each—and there were so many of them—was something I used to marvel at.

I will never forget one of his employees coming in with *laddu*, an Indian treat, which she presented to him in a Tupperware container. He asked about her father in detail, and as it turned out, he had reassured this woman, a young mother stretched thin, that while her father was ill with pneumonia and in the hospital, she was not to worry about missing work. While some bosses will say things along those lines, sometimes employees can tell that it's a rote statement and not the real truth. His employees, on the other hand, knew he meant what he said. He made real connections, and I aspired to emulate that type of leadership as I moved into positions where I led teams.

As a leader, I obviously motivate my team and help them create goals. But I can only do so by getting to know them, by valuing them, and by caring. Then as a leader, I help my people shatter their goals and form new ones. I like to think that I have taken a *lifetime* of an incredible work ethic as a student of both business and people, and I have crafted a style that is both straight talk and hard work, along with compassion.

But I think I approach goals and motivation with what I gained in the trenches of my career. To explain this, obviously as a C-level revenue executive, I'm extraordinarily financially driven. Math, money, finance, and hard work—that's my jam. At one point years ago, while working for a major global corporation in Chicago, my goal was to make six figures. I wrote it out as a sales goal. That year I came in at $91,000, and I was furious. Then I looked at my *actual* performance. I made the president's club, and I hit 165 percent of my goal. So how did I not make six figures with *all my hard work*, which I was hardwired to deliver and was passionate about?

Then I realized that it wasn't my performance; it was the environment I was in—I was never going to be able to reach those numbers I so aspired to. The goalposts had been moved, as they say. With the type of performance I delivered, I should have had *no* issues making my financial goal. However, the comp structure was set up in such a way that no one, no matter what they did, could reach it. That is not the way to motivate a sales team.

Thus, when it is time for my people to set their goals, I remember that inner fury I felt when I realized that the system was, in essence, rigged to make my goals unattainable. When I build my comp plans for my people, I give them "reach" goals—but if they are disciplined and willing to put in the hours and if they show grit, persistence, and determination, they can get there. I am cheering them on the entire way and imbuing them with self-belief. They also see *me* work harder than anybody in the room. (You can't be a leader if you don't set a clear example.)

Another aspect of my leadership style, and one of my father's powerful lessons from the past, is knowing my people. At this moment as I am writing, I have 130 people reporting to me. That number had ballooned to 400+ at my previous company. I like to understand their goals at the beginning of each year, and throughout the year I meet with each person four times.

But January goals are not enough. January goals are what everyone does, and most people fail at this. This book will show how to hold yourself accountable *quarterly* to win— and win big. We will, in fact, look at your goals and your plan in the very next chapter.

> **Hold yourself accountable *quarterly* to win— and win big.**

In addition, in my experience I noticed that most corporations have company goals; of course they do! But they have only *company* goals. Not on my teams. We have individual goals, team goals, *and* company goals. By meeting with my people one-on-one and putting in that face time, we are able to translate their goals into actionable steps. We find a reach—without it being so difficult to attain that it's discouraging and motivation busting.

The Five Questions

For our quarterly face-to-face, I typically give my people five questions. They all get the same five questions. It's in the invite; they know exactly what to prepare for. (I loathe leadership styles where you are on quicksand—always guessing at expectations.) Each question requires *radical self-honesty*. They are simple yet, if answered truthfully, will get at the heart of motivation and hard work.

1. What's working? (What's working for you, for the team, for the company?)

2. What could we improve upon?

3. What are your goals for the year? And then as we go through the year, how are we in terms of achieving them? Where can I help you? Where can your leader help you? (They all know these are not empty promises—I am there for them.)

4. What recommendations do you have for the business? You are in the trenches. Tell me something about our customers or about how we're doing things that you think is going great that we should expand upon.

5. The last one is open: What questions do you have for me? Nothing is off-limits.

Another thing I know about leadership is that you need to understand that you will hear things that might not thrill you when you ask for radical honesty. And that goes both ways. I tell my teams what they want to hear, what they need to hear, and what they can't stand to listen to. And I expect that same honesty in return. (Real leaders are unafraid to be challenged.)

One thing I notice is that some people will tell you what they want. And that may be to leave you: "I want to move into customer success" or "I want to be promoted into sales." For some leaders, that might seem like a blow. To me it means I have done my job as their coach. I have had years when nearly 40 percent of my people have been promoted. That's an unheard-of number. And this mama bird is OK with pushing her fledglings out of the nest.

What does that sort of support in helping people pursue their goals do? For one it builds loyalty. When I was at CareerBuilder, I had people with me for years. Sometimes I had people who then left to have children or to try something else—and they often came back. And I always welcomed them. I encourage my people to go and do what they are passionate about because passion will fuel hard work—whether that's working for me or working in a role that is next on their journey.

I think this idea of support is so important to me because I learned this approach in the trenches. I had a boss who held me back, and I was so extraordinarily frustrated. I worked for this person for several years. He knew I had taken a step backward in my career due to my life-changing accident (which I will discuss in more detail later in the book). I had worked over two years to take my team from the "Bad News Bears" to number one in the company, yet he did not want me to grow into the next leadership position and would submit his other leaders who had less-than-stellar results and never me.

When I moved into leadership positions, I was determined to be a different kind of boss. People from my teams will call me years later and tell me I helped them transform their career. That, in and of itself, is a powerful reward for my methodology. That "horrible boss" experience was not my first, nor was it even close to my last. But after that I always said to myself that I would never stop anyone from doing what they want to do, even if it hurts my part of the business.

I had one leader who had a baby. (I've had over twenty direct reports have babies. It's exciting!) She went on maternity leave, but when she came back, I was worried because she seemed stressed and exhausted. At that particular company, the maternity/paternity leave was not generous. I shut the door, and I said, "You're a new mom. I just want you to know that I trust you completely. If you have to get creative with how you get your work done, if you have to come in late, work a couple of days from home, and adjust your schedule to something that works for you, I do not care. You need to do what you need to do for you and the baby and your family." (This approach works if you can trust your team. As a leader, if you can't trust your team, you don't have the right team. That goes both ways. If your people cannot trust you as a leader, you're not the right kind of leader.) She ended up staying with me for three years. Then she wanted to go into more of a solution architectural role, which I encouraged and supported. And guess what? She came back to me a couple of years later.

Hope and Clarity

When I think about who I am as a leader, I think about *hope* and *clarity*. Here's how that sort of talk with one of my team goes:

My hope is you have the ability to do this. I believe in you, so this is my sincere hope. The clarity is that here are the expectations of the job and the goals we have as a team. If you don't perform, here are the consequences (because I never want you to have to guess). But my hope is we can achieve this together. You got this.

Looking back, I always approached my goals in life with hope. Furthermore, I reached for clarity in defining them. This attitude depends on a certain optimism that was ingrained in me when I was a child. Even though my parents *expected* me to keep my nose to the grindstone and to apply myself, I was loved. Hard work and expectations set me up for success; in turn, helping your child or team member succeed is love. This kind of love is related to compassion. "I think you can do this job; I hope you can. I know you have the ability to do this. So these are the things that you're going to need to do. If you don't do them, then you won't have the ability and tools to do the job. Or maybe this isn't the right job for you."

I have actually had those conversations over the years with my employees. As a result some have gone off to other positions or changed fields entirely. Later many of them have sent me notes. "Thank you for helping me find that clarity, my passion, and what I was meant to do."

Pursuing clarity extends to my coaching clients. Many are in sales, customer success, and solution consultant roles, areas in which I have excelled the most. One of the things I tell them is that part of working hard is taking the time to figure out what your game plan is and then relentlessly executing it. I'll give you an example.

Recently I was talking to one of the people I coach. Remember that I demand radical honesty. He said to me, "Puja, I'm stuck."

When I asked what was going on, he continued, "Obviously, I'm concerned about the economy, and I'm worried about retention. I feel like my people are putting in the work, but we are one month from the end of our year, and I am concerned we are not going to hit our number. We are close, but the stretch to get there doesn't look like it's going to happen, and I just don't know what to do."

He may have thought I was going to ask about leads or about the specific members of his team. But instead, my response to him was, "OK, but what are *you* doing exactly as a leader?"

"Well, I'm coaching them."

"All right, what are the top five deals in your pipeline?"

He rattled them off.

"And have *you* spoken to all those potential customers?" When he shook his head, I asked, "Why not?"

He explained that he was depending on his sales reps.

"Ah, but aren't you their leader? Don't you know this business and the sales better than anyone else?"

He said yes. (And I happened to know from our coaching sessions that this was true).

"Then why are *you* not putting in the work? Why haven't *you* talked to those five prospects? Your reps get it to a certain point. Your job is to take it over the line, to be closer."

He had a light-bulb moment. He had forgotten a very basic business truth: the 80/20 rule. He knew the rule when he worked for me before he moved on, and I eventually became his coach.

The rule is that 80 percent of your money comes from the top 20 percent of your customers. As the leader, you want to have a relationship with your top customers, period, end of story. That is because reps change, leaders change, and companies change. If you, as a leader, don't reach out regularly to your top 20 percent of clients, those clients may not know there's *always* someone there whom they can call. That's the hard work. Leadership doesn't mean all those basic rules and the discipline of hard work ease off as you supervise others. Leadership means you are like 7-Eleven—on call 365 days a year, 24 hours a day. *You* are in charge of the people in your care, and don't you forget it.

I teasingly joked with him. "Why are you forgetting all my lessons?"

He replied, "I don't know. That's why I called you!"

Hardwired to Work Hard Does Not Involve Being on a Hamster Wheel

Now I have another very important leadership lesson. What do tenacity and grit look like? Don't assume you know.

I am amused when CEOs or high-powered sales leaders show me their calendars. They tend to brag about how "busy" they are. Guess what? If your calendar is filled every second of the day, I'm sorry, but you're not working. You are not absorbing and listening if you don't even have time to eat a sandwich! Believe me, it's fine to have bouts of that. I consider the beginning and end of the quarter as those types of periods. But at the end of the day, *working hard means working smart.* That means that your calendar isn't filled for the whole day or twelve hours a day or fourteen hours a day. Instead, you're setting aside time to really think about your business, think about what you're working on, think about how you can improve it—and then go put in the hours to do it.

I coach my own people on this principle. But it's not enough to coach it. We *live* it. I actually believe that all my leaders need a Think Day.

What do I mean? The art of working hard includes giving yourself time and space to think. If you're constantly on a hamster wheel, you're working hard, but you are never going to level up. I make my leaders take one day a month off. I don't care what they do. But they need to *not* be on the hamster wheel. If they golf, I say, "Go golfing." If they like culture, I suggest visiting a museum or taking in a show. Or they could take their kids to the park—whatever it is that releases their mind from the grips of the rat race.

The art of working hard includes giving yourself time and space to think.

I do the same myself because if I don't stop and have time to think, I can't regain perspective. If I don't have a plan, then I cannot focus my hard work on a clear goal. Instead, someone else is owning my day. *Part of working hard is the ability to own your day.*

The Course Correction

So what does it look like when, as a leader, I have to help someone make a true course correction? I'm compassionate, but clarity means, again, radical honesty.

I had someone on one of my teams come in with his quarterly business report (QBR). The QBR, which all people who report to me or any of my leaders must prepare, shows what's in their pipeline. In walked someone I thought had all the potential in the world. But I—as a "facts and figures" woman, a C-level revenue executive—had a calculator. Once I crunched the numbers, I knew immediately that there was a disconnect between what the team member wanted to earn and his somewhat pitiful pipeline.

My talk to him went like this: "I think that you have the ability to be a star. However [by the way, I don't use the word *but* ever], this pipeline does not equal a star. So I need you to leave. You can go home today; you can go outside, go get something to eat. I need you to really think about why your pipeline is not that of a star. What do you need to do to improve?"

The word *however* to me is more open-ended. It implies hope. It doesn't shut anyone down.

I *hoped* he could become a superstar. Without anger and without shaming him, I offered *clarity* that things needed to change for that to happen.

Guess what? This past New Year's, I heard from this now superstar. He texted me that he and his wife bought their first million-dollar home. He added, "I want to tell you that this would not have been possible without your coaching way back when about my funnel. I walk into every QBR now knowing that I'm gonna slay it because of that feedback you gave me."

STRAIGHT TALK
FROM PUJA

As I wrote in the introduction, in every single chapter, I will challenge you right here, right now, to start to get it together. In this chapter let's look at our twin values of hope and clarity.

What is your *hope*? Now—straight talk—there is no room here for wishy-washiness. If you want to go for something, say it. If you have a "reach" sales goal, spell it out. What do you *hope* for? And if you accomplish that, what will it do for your life? So for example, if you want to earn six figures, will that get you into the dream house you want or allow you to travel? What do you hope for? Make it real.

I hate to break it to you, my readers, but hope alone is not a strategy. Now we need *clarity*. First, break it down. List one thing you can do *this week* to work toward your hope. Now do it. Pretend you are bringing me your sales goal or your career goal or your personal goal. What am I going to tell you? *Do it.* No excuses!

Are you a star? I think you are. If you bought this book, you obviously want to get it together and succeed. I believe in you. So you better also!

Here are your three challenges for chapter 1:

1. Define your *hope*—something that's a reach—in one sentence.

2. With *clarity*, name something specific you will do this week to move toward that.

3. Commit to reading chapter 2 this week.

CHAPTER 2

Get Set: The Plan

If you don't know where you're going,
you'll end up someplace else.

—YOGI BERRA

What are your goals? I *hope* they are lofty—big dreams that embody what you truly want out of life or the lifestyle you desire, the place you want to live in, the countries you want to travel to, or the career and job you are passionate about. I hope you have goals that take into account your health and well-being. I hope your goals fill you with excitement and ambition. That truly is my wish for everyone.

Now I'm offering a dose of clarity. Unfortunately, many people confuse goals with "the plan" for how to achieve them. In fact, there is a whole swath of the self-help segment, for example, that will have you create a vision board or meditate on your goals. They'll have you picture your goals—in great detail. And I think that's important. But what they don't do is prepare you to accomplish that beautiful dream.

We can begin by writing down our goals. Writing connects us to our goals externally—in other words we see it taped to our mirror or written in a journal or appointment calendar. It reminds us daily of what we are setting out to achieve. However, writing also connects us in a neuropsychological way to our goal *internally*—scientists call this encoding.[2] According to research, "Encoding is the biological process by which the things we perceive travel to our brain's hippocampus where they're analyzed. From there, decisions are made about what gets stored in our long-term memory and, in turn, what gets discarded. Writing improves that encoding process. In other words, when you write it down it has a much greater chance of being remembered."[3]

Yes, write down your goals. But if you want to *get it together*, if you truly want to embody the GIT mindset, you can't neglect the most important part. You cannot hope to achieve your goals if you have no actual *plan*. So let's roll up our sleeves. Here are some essential elements of "the plan."

Know Your Why So You Have Your Reason to Push Through

When I think back about my parents and how they committed to their plan to move to Canada and then the United States, as well as obtain their advanced degrees, I know that there were stretches when they were exhausted. By the time my mother graduated from school, she was rail thin from the hours she applied to both raising my sister and me and her studies and more. Both my parents, despite intense

---

2   Mark Murphy, "Neuroscience Explains Why You Need to Write Down Your Goals," *Forbes,* April 15, 2018, https://www.forbes.com/sites/markmurphy/2018/04/15/neuroscience-explains-why-you-need-to-write-down-your-goals-if-you-actually-want-to-achieve-them/?sh=7ae431eb7905.

3   Ibid.

careers and education goals, ensured my sister got to cheerleading practice and that I got to my sports practices (field hockey being one of them). Though that was years ago, working parents still face the challenge of needing to clone themselves to fulfill all their obligations. *So why keep pushing?*

I think for my parents, for me, for the people I coach, and for you, my reader, it starts with your *why*. Philosopher Friedrich Nietzsche wrote, "He who has a why to live for can bear almost any how." What that means, in a practical sense, is that there will definitely be times when life comes at you fast and hard. There will be times when what you are setting out to achieve might seem too far from your grasp, times when it gets terribly difficult.

It is at those moments when you have to recall your *why*. For my parents, as immigrants, it was to make a better life for their family. For you, it might be your partner, your children, a desire to purchase a house, a personal ambition to reach the C-suite. But it helps to really spend some time looking inward to figure out precisely *why* you are applying yourself, why you are persisting, why you are aiming high, why you have tenacity.

Hold that *why* close to you. Commit to it because when the grind times come—and they will—your *why* can remind you of the meaning of your commitment.

Make Your Goals Manageable

An extraordinary woman I know, every single New Year's Day, writes down her goals for the year, all one hundred of them. Now I'd like to know, who can *focus* on a hundred things? Even I—a driven multitasker, a coach with a keen sense of getting it together—cannot. For my friend, these hundred things cover everything from dieting to exercise to remodeling a closet to career benchmarks. She will be running from one to the other like a chicken with her head cut off.

Instead, I coach everyone to focus on three goals, maximum, at a time (sometimes less than that, but we'll discuss that in chapter 7). By having two or three goals, you will possess a clear-eyed focus that allows you to make strong decisions without waffling or doubt.

Focus on three goals, maximum, at a time.

We are all bombarded by choices. Every single day, especially with our 24/7 connectedness mindset where we rarely shut off the noise of social media, texts, etc., our attention is divided. We sometimes feel pressured to make a fast decision on the spot when what we should be asking is, "Will this decision help me meet my goal?"

If the answer is no, then don't accept the social invite and instead focus on preparing for the big meeting tomorrow or on what you should be doing to develop your business funnel. Whatever choices you make in a given day, they should cut through the proverbial bullshit. Aligning all or most of your decisions around your main goal will help you *get it together*.

Set Goldilocks Goals

There are some of you reading this book who are checkmark addicts. What do I mean by that? You write long to-do lists, often with very easy, doable goals so you have the satisfaction of checking it off. You may be my readers who always got the gold star in elementary school. I know someone who puts "make my bed" at the top of her to-do list every single day—even though I don't think there's been a day she hasn't made her bed since fourth grade.

24

The problem with "too little" goals is they don't push you. You want *Goldilocks Goals*.

Goldilocks Goals are goals that are not *too small* nor *too big*. Manageable goals do not mean you don't stretch. Your goals should be ambitious. They should be a reach. They should challenge you. However, your goals should not be so big that you don't have an actual *plan* to get there. These would be like setting a goal of $2 million in sales when you've only ever brought in $75,000. Unless you have a clear plan for how you are going to ramp that up beyond even your boss's expectation, you are highly unlikely to attain such a leap of a goal. If you are one of those people who like the gold stars, then not reaching your goals at all is likely to discourage you. Discouraged people often just give up.

Goldilocks Goals, then, are goals that are "just right." This is an area where I work with my teams to ensure we are setting a vision for the year that pushes us—but also is not impossible.

Break It Down into Quarters

As you'll see in figure 2.1, you can fill in this Goldilocks Goals sheet—and you can duplicate it for different areas in your life. For example, as a fibromyalgia activist, I take my health very seriously, and I have lifestyle and wellness goals, such as ensuring I schedule my acupuncture sessions and take time to rest.

For our purposes we will use this form for your career goals. First, what are your overarching goals for the year? A certain promotion? A certain sales number? This should be a focused goal, maximum of three.

In the first-quarter box, you need to ask yourself what three actions and smaller goals you can do for the next three months to make progress toward your "brave intention" (in other words, that big goal you know you can attain if you focus and put in some grit and grind). Write those actions in the Q1 box. Put those brave intentions somewhere where you'll see them often.

Obviously, the first quarter ends in March. So in the first week in April, like clockwork, etched in stone (whatever cliché you want to use), it is time to look at what you did or didn't accomplish.

GOLDILOCKS GOALS

YEARLY GOALS

1.
2.
3.

QUARTERLY GOALS

Q1	1.
	2.
	3.
Q2	1.
	2.
	3.
Q3	1.
	2.
	3.
Q4	1.
	2.
	3.

Figure 2.1: Goldilocks Goals chart

Use Your Radical Honesty

We talked about having radical honesty with ourselves. The concept of radical honesty was first described by author Brad Blanton. It can encompass many aspects of honesty—but for our purposes, it means we're not going to tell ourselves little lies.

Think of a teen who really, really wants to be the lead in the school play, but they are passed over. They may tell themselves, "I actually didn't want the lead. It would be too much rehearsal time." That sort of lie about the goal itself is unhelpful.

Next, I teach my teams and those I coach to use a color-coded system. I have them highlight in green those goals they reached. Yellow are the ones they embarked on but they know they need to work more toward or expand upon. Red are the ones they didn't reach.

Now analyze the red. Ask yourself:

1. Does this goal still serve you? Maybe it doesn't—and that's OK as long as you are not shifting the goal because you are not willing to push yourself.

2. If the goal no longer serves you, how will that impact your year goals? For example, if your goal was to make a certain dollar amount of sales in the first quarter and you opt not to do a course correction, then is your financial goal or career goal for the year derailed? Are you willing to abandon the bigger goal?

3. If the goal still serves you, now it's time to do an in-depth analysis. Why did you not reach it? Where did you lose the thread? What did you neglect to do? What could you have done better? What did you do really well so you can build on that?

4. Rinse. Repeat. By that I mean you carry over any goals you did not meet in the first quarter (those in red that you intend to keep) or goals you need to expand (the yellow) into the second quarter. And then you repeat the same exercise at the end of the second quarter.

Avoid the New Year's Trap

My particular four-quarter methodology frankly comes from my experience of many years in sales and from my leadership of revenue organizations. I use this system with my reps for their quarterly business reviews.

If you go out walking in your neighborhood on January 1, I bet you'll see *many* walkers. By the third week in January, you'll see a handful. It's my number one problem with my teams, and I see it over and over again: people are fired up to make their beginning-of-the-year plan, and then by the end of January, the plan has been abandoned. It is the New Year's trap. People do it with health and weight loss goals, goals about eating better, goals about exercise, and goals in their relationships and in their careers. I see it. You see it. There's a reason the busiest months for gyms and gym memberships are March (people starting to think about bathing-suit season) and January. And there's a reason many people stop going to the gym before midyear even arrives. They have no detailed *plan* for how they are going to approach their goals.

When I meet individually with my teams, I make sure we look at each quarter through the lens of focus on those goals. I met with one of my favorite sales reps. He looked at me and seemed puzzled. Staring at his numbers in black and white, he asked, "Why am I only at 80 percent of my plan?"

I told him two reasons. They are the reasons I see over and over and over in people.

1. They are not doing weekly, monthly, and quarterly self-assessments. Without knowing where you *are* at all times, how can you possibly know where you are headed?

2. They have not done anything to get to those goals. They have merely done what they have always done. Maybe if the planets all aligned and you sprinkled a little pixie dust, you'd magically reach your goal. But to reach a "stretch" goal, you must do more than summon Tinker Bell. You need to take actionable steps.

You may recall from chapter 1 that I meet with every single person in my charge, from business development reps to sales leaders. Using the wonderful example of my father knowing everyone in the manufacturing plant he ran, I believe it is important that they have face time with *me* and that they know that, from the top down, they are known and valued.

Microsteps to Success

Microsteps are an essential component of *getting it together*. Microsteps are small, consistent steps that you take day after day that you may or may not see results from immediately. But over time, with consistency, they are a pathway to success.

Suppose you have never been an athlete or a runner—the most exercise you typically get is walking from your desk to the coffee machine—and you decide to run a marathon. You're not going to wake up the next day, go buy an expensive pair of running shoes, put them on, lace them up, and run 26.2 miles. You're going to look at the target date of your marathon and then work backward, creating a training regimen that likely will start with brisk walking, then jogging a little, resting some days, eating properly, and running short distances, then medium distances, then a half-marathon. Each day you would take microsteps. If you walked ten blocks on day one, by week two you might be walking fifteen. Each day you would build on the success and training of the day before.

Now in the spirit of radical honesty, I want to tell you something that many coaches will not reveal. (And I am going to set it off so you pay attention.) *Do not expect to be motivated every day to get out there and make things happen.*

Even at the intense levels at which I operate, every day is not pedal to the metal. We all have days when we are tired or coming down with a cold, nights of insomnia or family problems and concerns, and days when our confidence lags. We might have off days "just because." That's why motivation is not everything. *Discipline is.*

You cannot count solely on motivation to get you to your goals. You count on discipline.

You cannot count solely on motivation to get you to your goals. You count on discipline. That's what microsteps do for you.

Face it, if motivation was the only factor in reaching your goal, we would all be millionaires because we want to reach that financial goal, and we feel motivated (on January 1!) to achieve it. But very few people maintain motivation—and because they don't have discipline, they cannot count on microsteps to maintain momentum.

Microsteps versus Micromanagement

Microsteps apply to your career goals—and if you are a leader with people in your care, microsteps apply to how you lead and motivate your people and hold your team accountable. Many sales leaders think that letting salespeople run their sales however they want and just trusting them to do their job is going to work, and it doesn't. First, salespeople are often those with a very high emotional intelligence or with a high emotional quotient (EQ). People with a high EQ, a population studied in depth by psychologist and author Daniel Goleman, are those who work and play well with others, to use grade school parlance.

> *Emotional intelligence (EI) is the ability to perceive, interpret, demonstrate, control, and use emotions to communicate with and relate to others effectively and constructively. This ability to express and control emotions is essential, but so is the ability to understand, interpret, and respond to the emotions of others.*[4]

That "people person" trait of salespeople does not necessarily translate to high levels of discipline and organization. I really want my best people to be consistent. Therefore, I make their lives somewhat consistent. Every Monday is our Monday-morning huddle. Every Monday afternoon is a forecasting meeting. The reason I have it on Monday is that we need to know if we are good or in trouble. And if we're not good, then how are we, as a team and individually, going to *get it together*? On Tuesdays, Wednesdays, and Thursdays, my people

---

4   Kendra Cherry, "What Is Emotional Intelligence?" Verywell Mind, November 7, 2022, https://www.verywellmind.com/what-is-emotional-intelligence-2795423.

should have enough meetings scheduled to fill their pipeline. Fridays are a decompress day. I don't hold any meetings on Friday. However, anyone who wants to talk to me, wants my advice, or wants to bounce something off me knows that my schedule's always open on Friday for the most part.

This consistency offers my team the microsteps we need to be successful. It also provides support. For example, *no one* likes cold calls—no one. So we all suffer that misery together. I also try to gamify it; for example, I set contests consisting of prizes for the person who sets the most new meetings.

Now what is the difference between microsteps and micromanagement? Five little words: I am not a babysitter.

I provide structure. I provide motivation. I provide microsteps we can all embrace. But I cannot make anyone on my team perform.

Accountability Partners

When I set out to write this book, I knew my subtitle was going to be about "being the boss you need." I have never ever in my career led my teams by using fear-based motivation. I am going to be the one who *believes* in you.

But I'm going to hold you accountable. Without accountability it's much too easy to get seriously offtrack. This approach is not for me to micromanage or because I think it's oh-so-fun to ask my team detailed questions about their sales funnels. It's for them. And by proxy, as my readers, it's for you.

Here's a brief example. I had the honor of coaching a rep who had just finished being Rep of the Year. This was from a combination of hard work, a few "being in the right place at the right time" events, and a passion for what she was doing.

However, if you are in sales, you might know what I am going to say about the following year's goals. What generally happens when a rep or leader has an amazing year is they are looked at as a person who went from zero to hero the next year. And then if they don't follow up with an even-better next year, they go from hero to zero. It's because your quota is set based on last year's performance. People in sales can't win sometimes.

She brought me her goal sheets, and she opened up to me about the numbers that her company expected her to reach. She was overwhelmed.

So we focused, and we talked about how her biggest goal for the quarter would be to build her funnel. Excess meetings—decline. Too many social distractions—swipe left.

We looked at the funnel and broke down her year goal into quarterly goals. Then we took those and microfocused down to weekly. So far, so good. Now when you have a microgoal of, say, adding $50,000 to your funnel each week and one week you attain $70,000, then you know that if you have an off week, you are ahead of the game or at least breaking even. And if you have an off week, you know you must make it up the next week.

Got it. We were all on the same page—or so I thought.

At the end of the first quarter, she returned to me for coaching. Her numbers were horrifying. She should have had $600,000 in her mid-full. She was at $200,000.

I asked her why. She had some valid reasons. There were some big accounts that she was chasing that had not come in yet. But I'm not a coach, so you can tell me what I want to hear. I heard a lot of yada yada and blah, blah, blah. Guess what? Your accountability buddy should know how to cut through that.

I asked her to pull up her calendar. "Show me March, for example." It did not take long for me to see that every day there were three hours, sometimes four, without appointments, without tasks, with no clear agenda. "What are you doing in these periods?" I asked.

"I'm pursuing things. It's just not on my calendar."

I'm not going to tell you what year I was born, but I will tell you it wasn't yesterday. I was honest—not mean but *honest*. "This is the calendar of a 70 percent–ish plan, and most certainly it is not the calendar of a superstar—and I know you can be a superstar."

There is also the honesty of numbers. Numbers do not lie. Your results are there in black and white. This is an important concept as you will see when we talk about my "secret formula" for data analysis in chapter 6. The fact was she was seriously behind. Her new weekly and monthly goals for the rest of the year would need to reflect her early setbacks.

I also knew, as her accountability coach, that she could not afford to let another quarter go by with these sorts of numbers. I showed her how to block out those previously unclaimed, vague hours and transform them into calls and meetings with clients. Then I told her we would meet again in four weeks. It is so much easier to make transformations with some wiggle room than when you are feeling desperate. The sooner you reevaluate the better.

I will let you know that she made most of her goals—and instead of going from hero to zero, she remained in the top five, which was terrific considering the goals they had for her.

One of the things about being an accountability partner—or the boss you need—is that so much of success is activity based. They are risky investments—a series of work actions that have no immediate or guaranteed reward. No one wants to hear that. No one wants to do it. Building the pipeline is the worst, most miserable part of the job.

We all know grit and grind are part of the secret to reach the top. But very often people don't like to look too closely at what that means.

The Five-by-Five Strategy

Now a brief aside—I love tech (sort of). And I have people on my team who use tech *brilliantly*. However, the problem now is everyone uses technology, and no one wants to pick up the phone. That makes building those sales funnels even more difficult.

I have a friend who hates the phone. The world would have to literally be ending before she would even *think* of perhaps answering. (And then it would be a maybe.) But then again, she now hates texts. Since no one can get her on the phone, they text her. So when that blows up with too many messages, what's next?

Today it is very difficult to get through to people because of gatekeepers, modern tech, and our evolving attitudes and habits regarding how we communicate. But I tell my team to use the five-by-five strategy. It can look differently for each attempt, but here's a hypothetical.

A sales rep reaches out

- on LinkedIn (a personalized message),

- via a personal email,

- with a phone call (which likely will not be answered, but you can leave a message—try not to sound like every single salesperson on the earth, but get your pitch's points across),

- with a text follow-up if a contact has been made in person or over the phone, or

- via the method most likely to get to them.

Most people no longer answer their phones unless it is a number they know or are expecting. However, just as commercials you hear over and over again on the radio or TV will build familiarity with a brand, you are trying to lay a foundation of name recognition associated with *positive persistence*.

I think, because of the isolation many of us felt during the height of the COVID-19 pandemic, some people missed that human connection. I noticed that more people actually answered their phones and responded to messages during that time. But no matter how you reach out, even if it's uncomfortable, it has to be done.

Revenue Is a Formula

Few people understand, really understand, that revenue is a formula. And a formula is just a business way of saying "a plan." That's why consistency is the key to winning the game. All problems in revenue are solved by pipeline. Sales is a formula. I have talked to and coached so many start-up VPs of sales, and at the talk of a plan, sometimes I see their eyes glaze over.

However, all the comp plans, all the various deal structures, everything a sales leader might consider all boils down to that pipeline. I think sometimes leaders are afraid to tell their sales teams that it's about that pipeline because the nuts and bolts, the day-to-day consistency, don't sound exciting. It sounds like work.

But you need to change that mindset, or you and your team will not win. Instead of moaning about the "suck" of calls and appointment setting and following up on leads, you should be excited. Excited about cold-calling? Yes! Why? Because since that is one of *the* secrets of the formula for revenue, it means the code can be cracked.

Think about it. If no one could ever figure out how to successfully sell and drive revenue, it would mean it's a secret sauce, like on the Big Mac. No one's quite sure what's in it. However, if the formula can be spelled out, then that means *anyone* can crack the code with putting in the hours, grit, and discipline. That's great news!

Embrace the Suck

The military coined the term *embrace the suck*. I'm no drill sergeant. I'm the boss you need, and I am here to tell you that embracing the suck is just part of the job—every job.

I will say to my team, "Today you're going to do your calls part of your outreach sequence. And this is going to suck. No one likes cold calls. You're going to be dialing to get mostly voice mails. That's OK. Leave a voice mail. Leave your pitch."

Then we'll examine what it is we all dread about sales calls. If someone does answer a phone and snaps, "Not interested"—*click!*—I promise that you will live. Remember these four principles:

1. Don't take it personally.

2. They don't know you.

3. They won't remember you.

4. And since they won't, you can try again next week.

True story: if it makes you feel any better, I get a gazillion emails and calls a day. (Is gazillion even a real number?) A *lot*. Sometimes I pick up by accident, and if that person calls me again tomorrow, it would be like a brand-new call for me because it's one of a hundred.

And most importantly, if you have a day of hang-ups, voice mails, and disappointments, go back to your fundamentals. You do not waver on them. This brings us to our next chapter—"Relentless Execution."

STRAIGHT TALK
FROM PUJA

As I told you in this chapter, I don't have a hotline to Tinker Bell to magically conquer all my goals or for my team to reach and surpass all their sales goals. Here is the cold, hard truth: it takes grit and discipline.

First, you need to know what you are working *toward*. I'd like you to take the time to fill out your quarterly objectives from figure 2.1. Now keep in mind these three principles:

1. Have a big, brave, "just right" Goldilocks Goal.

2. Formulate the plan.

3. Swipe left for everything else.

I have another new concept for you. Aside from radical honesty about yourself, your goals, and your habits, you need to ruthlessly guard your goals and plan. I look at it almost like a marriage or partnership. If you don't protect what is special between you and your partner, it's easy for your relationship to derail. The same thing applies for a goal. If you too often say, "Just this once, I'll skip my outreach sequence," next week it will be easy to say the same thing. And then before you know it, you'll have a 70 percent–ish plan and not a superstar plan.

As you look at your goals, consider what the noise in your life is. What are the things you need to eliminate and tune out to clear the way to your goal? It could be that you need to cut down on your "work hard, play hard" approach, with too much playing occurring. Maybe you need to add discipline to your household—if every Sunday night looks like madness with you, your partner, and your kids running around disorganized instead of reviewing the upcoming week's goals and schedule, you are starting each Monday already behind even if, to you, it looks like you are keeping up. Look at your social obligations. Consider if there are relationships that are problematic with people who aren't supportive of what you want to achieve. Only you know what the noise in your life is. But if you are radically honest with yourself and then ruthlessly guard what you need to do, armed with the discipline and a plan we discussed in this chapter, there is no reason you can't achieve everything you set out to.

Here is your assignment for this chapter:

- Write out your *why* in the form of a single sentence—and then put it somewhere you will see it often.

- Ask what the three microsteps are that you can consistently do to reach your goal.

- List three distractions you need to avoid or eliminate to stick to your plan.

CHAPTER 3

Go: Relentless Execution

No such thing as spare time, no such thing as free time, no such thing as downtime. All you got is life time. Go.

—HENRY ROLLINS

It's wonderful to speak of mottoes and mantras, but results are what get you over the finish line. There is a big difference between "dream of it" and "do it." A chasm of difference also exists between "trying" and "results."

Let's unpack that for a minute. If you say you're going to "try to show up at the concert," you have already *built into* your statement the chance of failure—of not showing up. If you say you're going to "try" to cook Julia Child's beef Wellington for your dinner party, it sounds like you and your guests could possibly end up eating takeout Chinese food. Either you do something or you don't.

So in terms of *getting it together*, now it's go time. First, let's define *relentless execution*.

To be relentless is to keep going, no matter what, without stopping or easing up. It's never giving up. And it also usually implies a very high level of intensity.

The other half of this concept is execution. *In other words you can't be all talk, no action. It's not "trying"—it's doing it.*

If you build on each chapter of this book, you have goals and a plan (broken down into quarters). Now you have to pursue the goal and execute that plan without giving up.

> **Intuition is critical in virtually everything you do. But without relentless preparation and execution, it is meaningless.**
>
> **–TIM COOK**

So how do you "go" in the Get It Together mindset?

Start with the Basics

First, you cannot go or execute anything if you have no plan. So if you didn't complete your chapter 2 assignments, you're skipping an essential part of this success program. Go do it! (The correct response to that is, "Yes, boss.")

To me, starting with the basics means getting in touch with those qualities and traits that are the building blocks of success. These include the following:

- Grit. Determination. Resolve.

- No shortcuts. Realize there are none. You're running a marathon, not a sprint.

- Persistence. Don't be a January Firster. Persist through all four quarters year after year. (That's the relentless part.)

- Work ethic. You see the value of hard work. It's part of your makeup. (If you are from a family like mine, it's in your DNA.) You would never think of slacking—it's not in your nature.

- Discipline. This is different from persistence. Persistence is keeping at it no matter what. It's a mindset. Discipline includes the actual rituals, habits, and day-to-day actions that will lead you to your goals.

The basics will lay your foundation. Until you find that fire within and that grit, you won't be able to execute your ambitious plan.

How Are Your Habits?

Goals and habits go hand in hand. You can't "go" without good habits. This is the discipline part.

When people meet me, they see a leader, someone who can get up in front of a room and motivate a team. Those moments in the spotlight or interacting with peers at all levels of business can be deceiving. What others do *not* see are my habits. They do not see the amount of prep I do for the week for meetings. They don't see my healthy habits. They don't see my discipline. It's like that iceberg. You only see the tip, not what's under the surface—which is so much more than what is visible.

Let's take a look at your habits. How are you setting yourself up for success? Think of my piano student who did not practice. Without discipline and good habits, becoming a pianist is impossible. The same is true in sales—you can't become a superstar without superstar habits. So if you want to run with the big dogs, it's time to cultivate the habits to get you there.

First, how do you approach each week? Since the global COVID-19 pandemic, I think work habits have shifted because of working from home or hybrid working situations. Schedules are a little more fluid. But whether you do this step on Sunday night or Monday morning, set the right intentions for the week. Some people will think that because they are on that hamster wheel or are perpetual motion machines, they must be working hard and accomplishing a lot.

I hate to break it to you. While, yes, working hard is important, what's equally or more important is working *smarter*. You should have a plan for your goals using our four-quarter sheet. But breaking down those goals into real, actionable steps that you can take *every day* is essential. So on Sunday night, you should not only look at your calendar and your tasks for the week but also be centering yourself, thinking about the big picture, and doing all the things that will set up your week for exponential success.

Those tasks will look different for everyone, but they can include planning your work wardrobe and ensuring you have everything to get ready each day without wasted energy hunting down the right tie or shoes; meal planning; ensuring your kids are also set up for success with any papers needed in their backpack or folder, lunch is made, bedtime is enforced, etc.; reviewing your calendar in detail, mentally confirming you have everything you need for every meeting or for work-related travel; creating a list of calls that you need to make; and any other work preparation tasks.

Some people I know create an action list each weeknight for the next day. Others write down everything they know they need to get done for the week. By writing a list, it saves them from losing threads and forgetting minor tasks that can snowball and create problems if undone. It also frees their mind for big-picture thinking by listing all the "little" stuff so it no longer takes up space in the brain or short-term memory bank.

A second and important habit is ensuring you are making conscious choices to thrive physically and mentally. Successful people prioritize self-care (women are notorious for being last on their own lists—working moms even more so), such as exercise, healthy food, hydration, meditation, etc. We will get into mental healthcare in the "Be a Fighter" chapter, but suffice it to say, the pandemic really exposed issues related to coping and mental health for many people. As I have briefly mentioned and will cover a little more later in the book, I have fibromyalgia and rheumatoid arthritis, and these conditions reared their ugly heads after a car accident. When you are forced through circumstances to coexist with a chronic illness, you learn to stake out a claim for your own health and protect yourself by learning what works or doesn't for you.

Successful people prioritize self-care.

I make no *apologies for taking care of myself. You shouldn't either.*

The third trait I tell people to embody is the swipe-left mindset. We discussed this in chapter 2, but when I use that expression, I mean cut out the noise and the unnecessary in your life. Ask yourself, "Is this helping me get to my goal?" Another good question to ask is, "Will this be important a day, a week, a month, or a year from now?" Learn how to prioritize what is essential and shed what isn't.

Cut out the noise and the unnecessary in your life.

Fourth, learn the word *no*. Once you do learn how to swipe left, next learn to say no without apology. I feel no need to explain myself when I turn down social engagements. I don't feel I need to have an excuse to have a Think Day. *No* is powerful, and if you are executing your plan, you should have a laser focus on your goals and deny the intrusions.

Finally, as a coach, I teach my team members how to conduct their own postgame analyses. Think of it like the coach in the locker room after a football game showing players films of the game so they can point out ways to improve.

Self-assessment is a trait you can learn. It's also not just "conceptual." In other words, yes, assess how hard you worked or how you did with your commitment to work out each day before work. However, numbers don't lie. Track your data—and track it closely. (We'll discuss this in more detail in the chapter "The Winning Formula.") This ensures you can see when you are slipping and when you can celebrate your wins.

The Four Pillars

When I became the chief revenue officer (CRO) at a tech start-up, my first assignment was to establish organizational efficiency to then increase productivity. We also needed improved customer onboarding. Oh, and in my nonexistent free time, I had to produce our budget and quotas, and frankly, it was like Dante's third circle of hell.

It would have been easy, under the circumstances, for me to be completely reactive. I could have been just putting out fires—racing from one crisis or deadline to the next. However, being reactive takes away the benefit of calculating the most intelligent path—because being reactive necessarily involves an emotional response.

I utilized a four-pillar approach (see figure 3.1). For each pillar, tasks and data were broken down into minute detail—and my intention was to start on January 1 with fully formed plans for my team. There would always be a million other things to do as a new chief revenue officer, so I had to exercise my swipe-left mentality. We needed to be ready to *go*!

Each of the pillars was extraordinarily detailed. I spoke plainly to my team. "If we don't have the pillars laid down in a very short time, we will be in significant trouble."

Having the pillars was important to avoid something I have mentioned before—the "chicken with its head cut off" mentality. For instance, have you ever seen a toddler at a splash park running from spot to spot, trying to catch where the water is going to spout out next? That's how you will look if your approach is reactive: chaotic and without a *plan*. The four pillars afforded us a vision of what we needed to accomplish—together.

Relentless execution depends upon a vision and a plan. To give you a real-life example, when I presented the pillars, no one agreed with me. My team had thoughts about my approach. I listened, several team members presented solid arguments and ideas, and we found a meeting place in the middle that still got us to that "triangle" goal at the top of our pillars.

I want my people to argue with me. I truly believe that a key sign of a leader is when you have people who work for you that disagree with you and feel confident about telling you so. It is sometimes in the heat of the kitchen that the best meals are prepared. Without the freedom to alter the plan on the basis of team feedback, you can never execute. *Remember that radical honesty goes both ways.*

The bottom line is the plan you came up with in chapter 2 can change—but the principles of grit and persistence do not.

By the way, pay close attention to that data pillar. Approximately 70 percent of a company's data goes unleveraged.[5] Not on my watch.

Figure 3.1: The four pillars of revenue growth

ADAPT THE PILLARS

You can use the plan of the four pillars in other areas of your life. Whether you have a financial goal, a career goal, or a health goal, you need to identify the pillars that are going to support you as you move toward your ambitions. For example, the pillars of a health goal might

---

5   Tim Cassidy, "Data Driven Success—Revenue Growth Strategies," GDS Group, May 18, 2022, https://gdsgroup.com/insights/article/data-driven-success-revenue-growth-strategies/, accessed December 1, 2022.

include acupuncture and traditional Chinese medicine in one pillar, a commitment to going to bed early and sleep hygiene in another, a vegetarian diet in a third, and yoga classes three times a week in the fourth.

"No Excuses" Zone

You will not find a boss who fights for her team more than I do. But don't come to me with weak excuses either because I will call you on them. And just so you know, I don't let myself off the hook either. I expect my husband, who is my ultimate sounding board and best friend with great instincts, to call me out if I offer excuses myself.

However, seeing my parents' path when I was a child and teen taught me that excuses are a sorry way out of accepting personal responsibility. My mom, as she pursued her advanced degree, could have easily said, at any time, that lack of sleep, full-time parenting with going to college, and more were the reasons for not doing well in school. But it would never dawn on my mother or father—or me or my sister—to make those sorts of apologies.

I've heard it all: hiring freezes, macroeconomic conditions, onboarding or tech problems, my dog ate my forecasting reports, I was abducted by aliens. But usually when I look closely, it's because the plan was not correct or laid out in the first place.

Here are some reasons people make excuses:

1. They are unwilling to go outside their comfort zone. You cannot hope to achieve the successes you want without reaching. And reaching involves stretching yourself.

2. They are afraid, whether that's afraid of looking foolish or afraid of trying for fear of failing.

3. They have no goals. Without goals, people languish—doing the same old, same old without making progress or evolving and growing in their role.

4. They are unwilling to hold themselves accountable. If you don't demand the best from yourself, who will?

What about When You Hear the Word *No*?

No one, especially in sales, likes to hear the word *no*. But it is part of the job—part of *any* job. Relentless execution means the word *no* is not a brick wall. You can climb over, tunnel under, or walk around it—you just have to know how to handle rejection.

First, what kind of no is it?

- No for now. This kind of no leaves the door open. It's a no because it's not the right time or expense for the company at that moment—which does not mean forever.

- The mysterious no. I don't mean a mystery as in *The X-Files*. I mean you, as the salesperson, do not have enough information at the moment to know *why*. You cannot respond to this sort of no until you learn more about the company you are trying to sell to or the person you are trying to connect with. It's a no—that, with the right information and response, could turn to a yes.

- The maybe no. This is a no where a specific reason has been cited. It could be there is a concern that you can respond to, and then the maybe could become a yes.

- The *no!* This can be the "rude" no, the "stop bothering me" no, the no that is absolutely, 100 percent a no. (One thing to keep in mind is this could still be a maybe or a no for now. I have been in sales leadership long enough to know that the C-suite changes, companies are acquired, people leave, and new leadership comes in. You cannot ever assume that this *no*, no matter how vehement, is permanent.)

If you are interested in relentless execution, you need to be ready for noes. Here are a couple of strategies for handling the negative responses:

- Get used to it. After you have had a no, a no, another no, and one more no, chances are you are on your way to getting used to no. Talk to your peers. Talk to your mentors. Everyone has heard the noes—and you just need to accept and reconcile with yourself that this is an element of sales/your career.

- Do not take it personally. This goes hand in hand with getting used to it.

- Ask questions (unless it's a *no!*). Anything you can glean can help—if not with this account, then with your sales pitches and approaches in the future.

- Pivot. After you've asked questions, it might be time to pivot. Maybe your approach needs tweaking. Meet with your mentor, your teammates, or your boss. Figure out the whys of the no and how to respond.

- Remember, it's a numbers game. I am sure you have heard many variations of this concept. If for every ten doors you knock on you get one yes, then any noes are just stepping stones on the way to your yes. Just keep at it. (Relentless execution!)

- Go back to your plan. Years ago I had a sales team member who reminded me of Chicken Little. Every no brought out hand-wringing and panic. I had to remind him that the *plan* was nonnegotiable and to not lose sight of it. If your plan is sound, believe in it.

- Do not allow noes to derail your self-confidence. A no is just that, a no. It's that simple. It's not personal, nor should that no impact your self-belief.

STRAIGHT TALK
FROM PUJA

All right, no one's *handing* you anything. You and only you are the one who needs to get it together. So let's recap.

In chapter 1 it was time to get on our mark. We entered the right frame of mind by talking about working hard, persistence, putting the work in, and putting your nose to the grindstone.

In chapter 2 we devised the plan. We were getting set. Necessarily the plan included your goals, and we broke it down into quarterly objectives.

In chapter 3, with the plan and a commitment to pushing yourself and persevering, you are now ready to go! It's time for relentless execution.

These three chapters work together to help you develop momentum. It can be very exciting to see your progress, and ideally you will just keep building on your strengths.

Let's look at your three practical assignments to complete for this chapter:

1. Determine a habit you need to adopt and commit to it for a quarter (three months). To adopt a new habit takes sixty-six days, to be exact.[6] This habit could be setting aside time each Sunday night to plan your week, rising thirty minutes earlier each workday to make time for a walk/thinking, making three extra cold calls a day, or writing down each day's to-do list. (Remember from earlier in the book that writing down objectives helps encode them into your brain.)

2. Determine a habit you need to shed and commit to it for the next quarter. This might include only socializing once a week, giving up alcohol or another negative health habit, not being chronically late (gamify it—if you are on time every workday for a month, you might treat yourself to something special), not mindlessly scrolling on social media, etc.

3. Look at your goals from chapter 2. Determine which one you want to focus on and create a four-pillar visual for yourself.

Look, greatness takes work. But you didn't pick up this book to "kind of get it together." You picked it up so you can pursue exponential success. So don't skip these assignments.

Next, we'll learn how to be a fighter because there is no way to get it together at the level at which I want you to succeed unless you have some fight in you.

---

6 John Grohol, "Need to Form a New Habit? Give Yourself At Least 66 Days," Psych Central, October 7, 2018, https://psychcentral.com/blog/need-to-form-a-new-habit-66-days.

CHAPTER 4

Be a Fighter

**Wonder Woman is a fighter, better than most,
but it's what she fights for that is important.**

—GAL GADOT

Inside every one of us is a fighter. (Cue up *Rocky* theme song.) Some of us may have to wake our fighting spirit up. Mine is always awake—and my internal fighter is pretty outspoken and pretty tough. That fighter has learned through sales calls that went well and didn't, through leadership successes and doubts, through being that daughter of an immigrant family expected to work very hard for success, and through being a fibromyalgia "warrior" how to stand up not just for myself but also for the people in my care.

As we'll see in this chapter, being a fighter doesn't mean coming out wildly swinging and aggressively confronting every situation. Being a fighter is about analyzing the situation and figuring out who, what, and why you are fighting—and then applying all your energies to the correct challenge.

The Battle of a Hundred Million

First, before I get into my business battles, I have to share about being a different kind of warrior woman. Currently there are roughly 135 million people in the United States with a chronic illness of some sort.[7] For many, that battle is hidden. I am one of those hidden fighters—only, as you might expect from reading this book, I am not content to stay hidden or to give up.

The short version of my story is this. I was a passenger in a car on my way to travel for work. It was in Chicago—in light snow (so happy I live in Miami now)—and a truck hit us. I remember the impact, but I considered it a minor accident. The airbags didn't even deploy. I felt that sort of deep muscular ache that someone in a fender bender might experience, but ever the fighter, I shook it off—or thought I did. I had nine meetings set up! I had no time to go get X-rays or even to slow down. After all, I had been raised in a go-go-go, achieving mindset and family by amazing parents who kept up schedules, educational studies, and travel commitments that many people would find overwhelming. Yet I thrived (or thought I did) on that pace!

I called my husband, who urged me to go to the hospital to be checked out. But I basically sloughed it off. I continued on to the airport, and my flight was delayed. Actually, at the time, I thought that was a small blessing, as it would give me a chance to collect myself after the accident, to grab a cup of coffee, and to check my emails. (My phone is an extension of my hand!) As I was walking to the gate, I suddenly couldn't feel my arms or my legs anymore. I called my husband a second time, and I was soon on my way to the

---

7   "The Growing Crisis of Chronic Disease in the United States," Partnership to Fight Chronic Disease, accessed December 10, 2022, https://www.fightchronicdisease.org/sites/default/files/docs/GrowingCrisisofChronicDiseaseintheUSfactsheet_81009.pdf.

emergency room to be diagnosed with serious disc issues in my back (two herniated discs and one fractured vertebra). I went to work the next day with a cane and a neck brace.

Now I might as well tell you, though this chapter is called "Be a Fighter," do not be like Puja—well, the Puja of that time. Heaven forbid I would have called in sick. One of the lessons of life and of this chapter is to know when to be a fighter—and to fight for your people and your goals as hard as you can. But the other is when to objectively step back and think, "Should I be in this fight right now?" I had not yet learned to discern the difference—and that without your health, you cannot be a fighter for any of your goals.

Thus, my medical and personal odyssey began. I went from doctor to doctor—nine in all—looking for answers to my chronic, agonizing pain, my exhaustion, the numbness in my arms, and more. Or perhaps more specifically, I was looking for answers I liked. In fact, according to the Autoimmune Association, people with autoimmune illnesses usually have a 4.7-year journey to get their diagnosis.[8] I was eventually sent to the Chicago Neuroscience Institute, a world-class healthcare facility.

I subsequently went to three years of physical therapy and occupational therapy. However, doctor after doctor told my husband and me that I was in complete denial. The "old Puja" was gone—and I needed to accept my new reality, according to them. Their advice was to take a work-from-home job in customer service, answering phones. I was offered pain medications for the daily agony of my not-very-happy body.

---

8   "Avoid Autoimmune Diagnosis Delay—Tips for Early Doctor Visits, but Most Important: Trust Your Instinct," Autoimmune Association, December 6, 2013, https://autoimmune.org/autoimmune-disease-diagnosis-delay-tips/.

For me, with the career I aspired to, after being a high-flying sales rep and also desiring to go into leadership, I couldn't see taking a job working from home, one that was not pointed toward my dreams. There is nothing wrong with that career—it just wasn't *my* career. I was used to being out there in the action. Now I needed to be a new kind of fighter.

I had a wonderful boss and a great employer at the time. They were totally willing to help me file for long-term disability—but for me, that was not an option because I felt I could work. I think I knew if I went on disability, I would never be able to return to my career. So I determined I just needed to learn a new way of doing "me." I needed to learn to conserve my energy and to make choices that best supported me, whether that was a combination of traditional and alternative medicines and treatments or making choices about socializing so I didn't overtax myself. I learned to set boundaries for myself, and I worked for a company that encouraged me to care for myself first and foremost.

I had setbacks and triumphs over the next year. One of my triumphs was becoming a writer and blogger for the *Huffington Post* as a chronic pain advocate. I wrote the blog because, as I started to learn more about hidden, chronic illnesses, I realized the chronic pain community, especially women, needed a fighter to speak up for us.

While my diagnoses are fibromyalgia and now rheumatoid arthritis, the hidden illnesses out there include lupus, Crohn's disease and other digestive illnesses, sarcoidosis, Sjogren's, and more. For most people with chronic illness and pain, it affects every aspect of their lives, ranging from exhaustion or being unable to "do it all" to sensory overload to pain that permeates through their whole body to mental health struggles like depression and anxiety precisely because their "old life" is gone and they must now learn to navigate a new life.

When I wrote my blogs and essays, I addressed things like how to talk to your family and partner about your illness and experiences. As I found my voice as an advocate and "fought" for more understanding of a problem that affects over a hundred *million* people in the United States, I received many emails from men and women who told me their marriage was saved because, after reading my pieces, they had a better understanding of what their partner went through. Many women sufferers, especially, wrote me that, at last, they felt heard.

The whole story of being a fighter was a lesson I realized I could apply to my life and career. My husband and I never took no for an answer. Every time we went to a doctor who told us, "No, she can't do that," my immediate response was, "Yes, I can."

I am sure every single person reading this book has a personal battle. Maybe it's a hidden one like mine. Or maybe you have to leave a broken marriage, or you have to cope with a quiet grief over a loss, or you have a complicated relationship with your own family or your in-laws. Just remember, you are not alone—no matter what the battle is.

Know Yourself

Doctors aren't God. They have spent decades learning and perfecting their craft. But they don't know the most important factor. They don't know *you*, and they certainly don't know you well enough to know who you are as an individual and how you truly are a fighter. My eventual saint of a rheumatologist always said I was his best example because my husband and I never gave up.

Your boss is not God either. (Well, I am a goddess, but you know what I mean.) Your boss can know your performance and numbers—

but they cannot know for sure how much fight you have in you. Only *you* know that.

As a leader, I have always strived, as I said earlier in the book, to truly get to know my team. I do want to know what is important to them, why they "fight," and what they hope to accomplish. I can offer them a road map. "You need to make twenty calls today and strive to get five appointments out of that." But I can't dial for dollars *for* them.

So it's important to know yourself first and foremost. *You* are the number one factor in whether or not you are successful.

Know Who or What You Are Fighting

Next, know who or what you are fighting. For me it was my *illness*. But it was also the establishment, the white coats who had a certain mindset of what a patient should look like—and most especially how a patient should behave.

At different points in my career, I have had other fights. I found, for example, financial malfeasance at one company, which I then had to clean up and correct. I have had bosses who didn't provide the tools I needed for my team to be successful. That meant I had to go to bat for my team.

Here's an example. At different times in my career, I have repped products that were fabulous. (I would not feel comfortable selling something I did not believe in.) But there have been times when clients were clamoring for a certain type of update. Tech, as we all know, updates and reinvents products at lightning speed. We needed updates and product add-ons to compete. So that meant, at the C-suite, fighting for the changes needed and advocating for what the customers and sales reps wanted. Spoiler alert: I got the changes—and the teams in question, as promised, delivered.

It's important to know who or what you are fighting. How many of us have watched a couple where one spouse has had a horrible day, and their coping mechanism or their way of dealing with it is to be ugly to their partner? The fight isn't with the partner but with whatever happened that day. Or maybe you have seen people in the workplace who would prefer to sit around and bitch about their supervisor or leader rather than work on the issues that are holding them back from success. The *fight* is still with yourself—making sure you are doing all the things needed to set yourself up for success (which, if you have been doing your Straight Talk exercises, you surely are, right?).

If you realize your fight is actually with your position or company or leader and you know you cannot effect the change you need, then you know it's time to move on. The same can be said for a marriage or partnership where there is abuse—whether that's emotional abuse, substance abuse, or financial abuse. If you've fought for the relationship but the other person is incapable of effecting real change, you may be in the wrong fight.

Know Why You Are Fighting

You also need to know why you are fighting. Everything else is noise.

Focus. That is one of the keys to being a fighter. I have aspired to be a vice president and then to attain a C-suite position for years. That was my goal. That was my fight. This enabled me to swipe left on any of the things that didn't matter to my fight.

Computer issues? Well, that sucks, and it might be a temporary setback, but is it worth raging at IT? Does that help the fight for my goals? No.

Gossip? No time. Obnoxious personality of someone on the periphery of my work sphere? I'm not arguing with them—especially if they literally don't know what they are talking about.

We often complain about social media—especially trolls. No doubt you have watched (or perhaps been that person) as someone takes on the "fight" to prove that troll wrong. I would never bother. That's not my fight. The energy I spend on that could better be spent on my real fight.

The same holds true "in real life." Before you go up in arms about something, pull out your goal list—which is supposed to have just three focused goals. Is whatever you are about to fight about on that list? No? Move on.

And now before I get bombarded with emails on my website, let me assure you that none of us should look away from overt racism or from someone being verbally abusive in the workplace to someone with no "power" to fight back or turn away from other nonnegotiables. But much of what we fight about isn't actually our fight. So know who and what your fight is with and why you fight.

Another aspect is really digging deep and knowing *why*. By that I mean, why did you set your goals in the first place? Your why needs to be intimately tied to your heart and soul as a person. I will discuss my whys later in the book, but my husband and I set ambitious goals for ourselves, for the *life* we wanted to lead, and for the things we wanted to accomplish.

Your *why* is your motivation. Let's take a minute to talk about motivation and its role in our lives, careers, and fight.

Types of Motivation

Depending on which social psychologist's theories you subscribe to, there are different forms of motivation—as varied as humans but with common elements.

EXTRINSIC MOTIVATION

Extrinsic motivation is just what it sounds like. This is motivation outside of ourselves. This could include (for students) good grades or seeking praise from our parents, teachers, bosses, and loved ones. But these are also the motivations many of us are familiar with in our careers:

- Money
- Prestige
- Fame
- Material possessions
- Lifestyle (vacations, dining out)

Extrinsic motivation is about achieving or receiving a reward of some sort. Rewards don't have to be promotions and raises. They can be praise.

Extrinsic motivation can also be about avoiding punishment. Let's use our school example—who wants detention? So this motivates you to turn in your homework assignments. In a workplace example, it may be that a layoff is coming up in your company, and you know the bottom 10 percent of producers are going to be out the door. That "punishment" can motivate you to push yourself and "fight" to keep your job and to not be in the bottom.

One last thought here is do not think of the motivator of "money" as simply how many zeros follow the numbers in your paycheck. Most billionaires will tell you that, after a while, money itself is meaningless. They don't want to be broke—but there's not much difference between having $3 billion and having $3.5 billion.

However, for most people money is the currency that *gets them* what motivates them. For one person it may be lifestyle as I've listed above. For someone else it might mean they can purchase their parents a condo, or they can do nice things for their children, grandchildren, and their friends. Keanu Reeves famously gave away $75 million of his *Matrix* money to the crew to thank them for their work on all the films.[9]

INTRINSIC MOTIVATION

The opposite of extrinsic motivation is intrinsic motivation. Intrinsic, just like it sounds, is *internal* motivation. There is no reward that others can see. You may be doing it because it is fun, exciting, challenging in a good way, or personally satisfying, or it just makes you happy. The reward is inside.

Here are some examples of intrinsic motivation:

- Volunteering at a food bank because doing so makes you feel good inside

- Learning a new language for the satisfaction of it

- Painting or pursuing a craft because you enjoy it, not because you intend to turn it into a side hustle

- Playing tennis just because you enjoy it

---

9 Katie Ann Vacarelli, "Keanu Reeves Generously Gave Away 75 Million of *Matrix* Earnings," WomenWorking, January 27, 2021, https://www.womenworking.com/keanu-reeves-generously-gave-away-75-million-of-matrix-earnings-to-crew/.

- Cleaning your house not because it's fun but because, at the end, you have a neat and tidy home, which is important to your peace of mind

In the workplace intrinsic motivation could be taking on a special project because you are passionate about it, not because it will immediately bring a return of a promotion or more money. It might also include mentoring someone because you want to pay it forward from when you were mentored because that feels "full circle" and satisfying.

WHAT DOES MOTIVATION DO FOR YOUR FIGHT?

How does motivation help you? Think back to a time when you were *not* motivated. Many years ago I was assigned a "busy work" project by a micromanaging boss who was in over his head and loved to assign compiling reports and figures—only to never use them to forecast or set goals. While I *did it*, I nearly fell asleep at my desk, and the days I was doing this stretched on. It felt like *Groundhog Day*. I would work all day with my coworker on these reports—and at the end of the day, it seemed like we barely got anything done, only to wake up, come to work the next day, and have to do it all over again.

Motivation can do the following for you:

- Get you revved up to complete a task or to make sales toward that big goal (even the cold calls, which you may hate!).

- Help you drill down on your goals. When you know what motivates you, it can make your goals crystal clear. "I need to make $200,000 in sales this month to earn the trip to Hawaii for the top producers."

- Give you fight in the form of determination and persistence. If you don't make that sale today, you are damn well going to make it tomorrow!

- Elevate your performance. When you care about a goal and you are motivated to achieve it, you're going to deliver your best.

GAMIFY IT

Gamifying is about taking a task and applying the elements of a game to it to make it more fun. Here are two examples.

1. This is a simple game example related to productivity. Suppose you have a tendency to get lost playing on the internet during the day when you should be doing your sales calls and outreach sequences. "Reward" yourself with a fifteen-minute (timed) social media break for every solid hour of calls. And don't allow yourself to cheat! Or if you are a procrastinator, what minireward can you offer yourself for accomplishing a task you have been putting off?

2. A more serious example would be to figure out your reward for hitting all your sales goals—would you take a trip? How would you celebrate? Your company doesn't have to be the only one to gamify your sales or targets.

3. Let's say you want to lose weight. I am all for body positivity, so obviously it's not that you have to—but maybe it's your goal. For every two pounds you lose, give yourself a cheat treat. For me it is always a glazed donut.

Who's Your Cornerman (or Woman)?

So many people around you have the ability to influence you—and most of it is not in a good way. It's more noise.

In boxing the cornerman is the trainer or coach allowed in the corner to support the fighter. They can only enter the ring during breaks, but they are there to help the fighter, to remind them to fight hard, to encourage them, and to patch them up when they're hurt. Everyone needs a cornerman (or woman!).

I am the cornerwoman for my team. They're my team; they're my people. I am ferocious in terms of protecting my people, and everybody, any team I've run, is aware of that. I know how to patch them up—how to motivate them when the fight gets rough or when they are discouraged.

But for me I have one person whom I talk to. It is my hope that you also have your trusted person, your cornerperson, the person you can be completely "real" with, the person who will call you on your nonsense and hold you accountable, the person who believes you are a champion. And my trusted person is my husband.

Before I met him, my father and I were driving to Chicago when I was relocating for a career opportunity. My father knows me so well (we are a lot alike), and he told me, "You have to find a man who's stronger than you."

My husband definitely matches my strength, and he is an extraordinary listener. And when I'm upset about something, 99.9 percent of the time, he asks me, "Why do you care?" (Know the why of your fight.) I feel very fortunate to have this type of relationship where I can continue to climb and continue to be a beast in pursuit of my goals, and I have someone who can help me focus down to the essentials.

There's No Magic Wand

Another important aspect of being a fighter is knowing there is no magic wand. No magic career fairy is going to come help push your career along. I've always found that it's really a conglomerate of individuals who will believe in your fight first and foremost. And then once they believe in it, they will help you get to the next level. But you have to be your own magic first.

There's no skipping over tough stuff.

Also, there's no skipping over tough stuff. There's no doing steps A, B, and C and then going straight to M. So when you set your goals, you need to get real about what it's going to take to achieve them and fight for them. Remember our Goldilocks Goals—they need to be ambitious but "just right."

When I have my quarterly meetings with my people, we may set sales goals, but I can't create opportunities for them. I may be their cornerperson, but I am not magic (well, maybe a little magic).

Goals + Fight + Consistency = Success

Goals must be wed to your fight—and you must be consistent. Remember, you don't want to be the person who sets ambitious goals on January 1, only to drop them by January 20 or to find yourself flailing in March.

"No magic wand" means there's no getting around that ambitious goals require fight. That's an important reason to know your why.

Self-Care Does Not Mean You're Not a Fighter

This is an incredibly important topic, and it will not be the only time I discuss it in the book. We will discuss self-care, mental health, and more later, but in terms of our fight, we need to establish something right now: self-care does not mean you are not a fighter! Read that again.

Think of the case of Simone Biles. She is the most decorated gymnast in *history*. Think about that. She is not just a champion, an Olympic medalist, and the most decorated gymnast on Team USA but also the most decorated gymnast *ever*. Her training regimen was seven hours a day, six days a week. (She took Sundays off.)[10]

What kind of fighter must you be to do that for *years on end*? Then think about the pain all elite athletes must go through—sprains, strains, breaks, and wear and tear on the body. At the 2020 Olympics, Biles, however, found her mental game was off. She could no longer visualize—and when she took off into the air, she lost the ability to know precisely where she was in her turns and twists. One false move on any of her events, and she could seriously injure herself—the kinds of injuries where people break their backs or suffer a fall that causes lasting damage for the rest of their lives. Simone Biles bowed out of a couple of events (ones she was expecting to win gold for)—she put her own mental health and self-care above all.

Just as when tennis champion Naomi Osaka withdrew from the French Open in 2015 because of bouts of depression where there was a furor, so Biles's "fight" could have been responding to the vitriol on the internet and the judgment of people. (Most of whom probably treated walking from the couch to the fridge as their own Olympic sport.) But instead, her fight was to treat herself with the care she deserved and needed.

---

10   HAO, "Simone Biles: Daily Routine," Balance the Grind, June 13, 2022, https://balancethegrind.co/daily-routines/simone-biles-daily-routine/#:~:text=%E2%80%9CI%20train%20seven%20hours%20a,home%20and%20have%20some%20lunch.

Americans are a decidedly "shake it off" culture. We celebrate people who work themselves to death and people who "push through" the most difficult of circumstances. With the worldwide COVID-19 pandemic, though, we began to see the cracks in this sort of mindset. During COVID-19 we saw the following:

- There was a 25 percent increase *worldwide* in depression and anxiety.[11]

- Among young adults, especially hard hit by the isolation, 25 percent reported substance use.[12]

- Among essential workers, 22 percent reported suicidal ideation.[13]

It's time we dragged this topic out of the closet. Recently a woman I was coaching reported in that she was feeling very overwhelmed. In addition to a job and being a wife and mother, she also was involved with several time-consuming organizations, none of which contributed to her quality of life or happiness. After our phone session, the lesson for her in terms of being a fighter is that sometimes it is OK to remove yourself from situations that just aren't going to benefit you or are detrimental to your psyche.

I think of it like the nine doctors I met over the years. I did not allow their declarations to destroy me. Sometimes fighting is stepping away because it protects you. Stepping away means full and total

---

11 "Covid Pandemic Triggers 25 Percent Increase in Prevalence of Anxiety and Depression Worldwide," World Health Organization, March 2, 2022, https://www.who.int/news/item/02-03-2022-covid-19-pandemic-triggers-25-increase-in-prevalence-of-anxiety-and-depression-worldwide.

12 Nirmita Panchall, Rabah Kamal, and Rachel Garfield, "The Implications of COVID-19 for Mental Health and Substance Use," KFF, February 10, 2021, https://www.kff.org/coronavirus-covid-19/issue-brief/the-implications-of-covid-19-for-mental-health-and-substance-use/.

13 Ibid.

elimination of the activities and situations that suck the life out of you and that are in no way, shape, or form helping you achieve your goals.

Blaze and Block

When we talk about the mindset of a fighter, sometimes you have to blaze your own trail, and you really can't worry about other people and what they think of you. Look, at the end of the day, it's not like I'm some superhuman jerk who doesn't feel emotional when people are upset with me. For example, when my team feels upset about something going on, that hits me hard because I think a cohesive team where we have one another's backs and best interests in mind is the best team for success. And to be honest, it's just painful when people we care about are unhappy with us.

But other judgment? I shrug it off. I know—with complete clarity—what I'm trying to do and what I'm trying to accomplish. So I use the block button.

You need to understand that when you blaze a trail, many people (including those who don't count) will have opinions. Here again is the double-edged sword of social media. What is designed to keep us close—to be able to follow our friends' lives and see their vacations or their kids in real time—can also be loaded with judgment. It's funny, but when I posted the press release about my book on LinkedIn, I was swamped with likes and comments—and many of the comments were from women who echoed that they felt like they needed this book.

I think that women, especially, play so many roles that it's a lot to deal with, and there are a lot of opinions. There are plenty of "shoulds"—what you should do as a mother or a partner in terms of work-life balance, how much you should weigh, what you should wear. Men receive judgment too.

When you feel the judgment as you blaze, then you block. *Always* consider the source and whether the person offering advice or judgment is worthy of listening to, knows your life in all its details, and indeed shares your values.

You can't let the nonsense and judgment that doesn't affect you take up space in your brain because your brain is like a machine. And the machine will be affected if you overload it. This will manifest itself in anxiety or stress, depression, or a host of physical illnesses.

With my own medical odyssey, believe it or not, there were some hidden silver linings. Because I was going through so much, my husband and I were forced to not be social. We were forced to only be able to do a certain number of things during a day, a week, a month. It was forced.

We had to make a very key decision. And our decision was either I would continue to focus on my career or we were going to have a social life. It was really one or the other. *That's clarity.*

Your One Thing

Oh sure, Puja. All this is great, but what do you do when everything is going wrong? When nothing you are trying in your career is working? When the proverbial you-know-what is hitting the fan?

First of all, I am a realist. If you are looking for me to spout a bunch of mantras and mottoes and just tell you to think positive, you bought the wrong book. I totally believe in spending time in thought (some might meditate), and I believe in thinking positive. But there's a tendency in our society to almost shame people for feeling defeated at times. People with illnesses are sometimes told if they just think good thoughts, the illness will go away. But the fact is we're all in this thing called life—and none of us get out alive. And sometimes life can be a real SOB. There's no sugarcoating it. And it doesn't help you, my readers, for me to speak in platitudes.

So when it seems like it's all falling apart, we drill it down. What's the *biggest* problem? I really have people focus on that when they feel like they can't keep fighting. It kind of reminds me of the scene in the original *Indiana Jones* movie when he's surrounded in the marketplace by numerous henchmen. He is vastly outnumbered. Then

Focus on the biggest thing they think they need to overcome to continue to fight.

the biggest, baddest assassin takes out a giant sword. And Indy shoots him. You need to figure out who or what the guy with the sword is.

With my people, I have them focus on the biggest thing they think they need to overcome to continue to fight. What is the one thing? I'll give you an example. One of my amazing leaders was building our customer success department from scratch. I was his partner in this immense project, but I was not the one actually building it. Instead, I would get him what he needed.

He came to me three months into the job. I looked at him, and I could see the distress etched on his face. He confessed, "Puja, I am so stressed out."

We broke it down. He had his people—check! He had much of the information he needed for one aspect of it, yes. But he moaned, "It's this 'customer life cycle' thing." He was having difficulty getting forecasting data from our retail side. He was also trying to build up the team and divide them between enterprise and midmarket.

So first, it was time for a deep breath. Then I said, "Here's what I think is the most important thing—the *one* thing—and tell me if you agree. I think that we have to get the structure of the customer success model built, and we have to start getting data because renewal season's coming in the next nine months. Customer life cycle is important, but it's not the number one thing right now."

He totally agreed. I suggested that we push the customer life cycle aside—for now. We could revisit it during the summer, which is when our business slows down just a bit. But our one thing was we could not lose any customers—that was our bottom line.

The problem was that no one can do five hundred things at a time. What he needed to do was narrow his focus—fighting for *one* thing, which was getting customer success up and running and getting our data that could help him do so.

As soon as I helped him focus on his goal, his shoulders relaxed, and the color came back to his face. And within forty-eight hours, he was "Slacking" me with new fight and energy.

When you focus on the one right thing, it doesn't matter what is swimming around you. I have taught all my people that "swipe left" should be your most favorite thing. What is going to happen to you? Is someone going to reach out and confront you over not responding instantaneously? Cool. I'm going to fight for you and tell them exactly why you didn't respond to them in a nanosecond.

And just so you know, I take my own advice. Look, I know there are other authors out there who talk a good game, but I don't know if they always take their own advice. I don't just take my own advice—I live it.

There were times, right after my accident, when I was in a neck brace, and I needed my husband to dress me in the morning. There were times when I didn't even have the energy after a long day at work to brush my teeth. When life gets that difficult, you have to be crystal clear about what your one thing is. All I'd ever wanted to do was be a vice president—since I was very young in my career. So suddenly, I was walking with a cane, but I was striving to still hit a hundred percent. I think most people would have crumbled. But it boils down to being hardwired for hard work that propelled me—and knowing how to focus on the *one* thing.

Remember your goal setting. I always have *one* goal (this could be as simple yet important as committing to seeing my acupuncturist weekly)—a singular personal goal to focus on. *One* goal is professional—what I aspire to that quarter. *One* goal is money related—a reach goal for saving, investing, or earning.

Stress toward a goal is different from stress on your shoulders. It's been many years since I had to worry about paying my bills. That kind of stress is indeed a grind. But the sort of stress I'm talking about is a *striving* stress. It's different.

One last word on your one thing: hopefully, when you set your goals, it will no longer be (if you used to do it this way) a list of a hundred aspirations. "I want to lose thirty pounds. I want to plant an organic garden. I want to take up yoga. I want to learn a new language. I want to … I want to … I want to …" There is nothing wrong with wanting to live a full life and aspiring to accomplish and explore many wonderful hobbies, healthy choices, and more. But if you want to *get it together*, then your fight has got to be focused.

You Have Permission

There's a famous saying. "It's easier to ask for forgiveness than it is to get permission." In my experience everyone's looking for permission because they don't know who to go to in order to get permission. And they're not strong enough to give it to themselves.

So this is your permission. It's all right to

- swipe left,

- transform your life,

- leave a job you loathe,

- leave a relationship with a past-due date,

- decide to go for that promotion, and

- fight like hell for your sales goals.

Whatever your dilemma or fight, you have permission to *decide* and then to go for it.

Roar of the Beast Mode

I have always joked that I go into beast mode when I am pursuing my goals. Then I realized it wasn't a joke actually. That beast mode was a mindset that I celebrate. Let's define it:

Roar of the Beast: a person who is extremely talented at whatever they do and always displays great determination, dedication, and resilience to always win or want to win.

Roar of the Beast is a mindset that, once you get used to accessing it, becomes part of who you are.

I think sometimes that ambition—and the determination, dedication, and *beast* mode that is required to pursue it—is sometimes given a bad rap. This is especially true for women. We seem to think going hard after something makes you cutthroat, perhaps even unscrupulous.

Get rid of that thought. You can be a beast at work, and you can pursue your goals—in a way that does not compromise your principles. No apologies needed for getting up each morning and roaring and going for it.

Beast mode is another way of saying you are "in the zone." According to Mihaly Csikszentmihalyi, "The best moments in our lives are not the passive, receptive, relaxing times … The best moments usually occur if a person's body or mind is stretched to its limits in a voluntary effort to accomplish something difficult and worthwhile."[14]

According to Csikszentmihalyi, these are the eight characteristics of flow:

1. Complete concentration on the task

2. Clarity of goals and reward in mind and immediate feedback

3. Transformation of time (It can feel like it is speeding up or slowing down)

4. Intrinsically rewarding experience

5. Effortlessness and ease

6. Balance between challenge and skills

7. Merging of actions and awareness, losing self-conscious rumination

8. Feeling of control over the task[15]

When you have the Roar of the Beast, you can have all those eight things going on—you can't be stopped. You're the boss!

---

14   Mike Oppland, "8 Characteristics of Flow According to Mihaly Csikszentmih-alyi," Positive Psychology, December 16, 2016, https://positivepsychology.com/ mihaly-csikszentmihalyi-father-of-flow/.

15   Ibid.

STRAIGHT TALK
FROM PUJA

All right, we've got to get you into fighting form. Time to get it together! (And you better not be cheating by skipping these exercises—not if you want to roar like the beast.)

1. Who or what is your biggest fight or battle right now in your career—and life?

2. Why do you fight? Zero in on your *why* and write it down.

3. What are your top three extrinsic motivators?

4. What are your top three intrinsic motivators?

5. How can you use your answers to questions 3 and 4 to gamify your goals?

6. Who is your cornerperson? How can they hold you accountable to your GIT goals?

7. What is the *one thing* you need to focus on right now?

8. Think back to a time when you were in beast mode. What does that look like for you?

GET IT
TOGETHER

Critical Thinking Is Underrated: Taking Time to Think

I try to encourage people to think for themselves,
to question standard assumptions.

−NOAM CHOMSKY

Spend some time on the internet, and you start to wonder if *anyone* has critical thinking skills. Critical thinking, in some ways, is very underrated. Remember when I said I like my people to take a Think Day? I don't know of any other boss who encourages that.

But it's more than just taking a Think Day. People seem to have forgotten how to check credible sources, access and understand data, and look at the facts. My father is a very analytical man. If I said someone at school told me something that was more opinion than fact (even a teacher), he would encourage me to check and confirm whatever it was myself.

We can define *critical thinking* as "a kind of thinking in which you question, analyze, interpret, evaluate, and make a judgment about what you read, hear, say, or write.… Good critical thinking is about making reliable judgments based on reliable information."[16]

Critical thinking has two parts to it: "1) a set of information and belief generating and processing skills, and 2) the habit, based on intellectual commitment, of using those skills to guide behavior."[17] So first, it starts with information, data, and fact gathering. Far too often in business, I have seen those "flavor of the month" sales leaders who, when sales get off track, throw a *lot* of spaghetti against that wall to see what sticks. Decisions made without data, without analyzing, without facts are decisions made in the dark.

Decisions made without data, without analyzing, without facts are decisions made in the dark.

The second part is definitely that commitment to critical thinking. I was blessed with parents who pushed their kids to think critically, and then I married a man who is the king of critical thinking. I don't know any other way to be.

Scaling Critical Thinking

Whatever business you are in, you didn't arrive on this planet knowing it inside and out. You learned it.

---

16   "What Is Critical Thinking?" Monash University, accessed December 12, 2022, https://www.monash.edu/learnhq/enhance-your-thinking/critical-thinking/what-is-critical-thinking.

17   "Defining Critical Thinking," Foundation for Critical Thinking, accessed November 22, 2022, https://www.criticalthinking.org/pages/defining-critical-thinking/766.

That is the amazing thing about critical thinking. When you have mastered that skill, you can apply it to your current career, job, and company—or the next one. Critical thinking allows you to replicate success, kind of like scaling a business.

My *first* presentation in my young career was to the CFO of Xerox. I was already a critical thinker—but I was too young and inexperienced to know I should have been nervous. Like every single career presentation of my life then and since, I was prepared and knocked it out of the park. It's not enough to *just* critically think—you have to then turn it into action or a plan.

At the same time that I was starting out there, I was being mentored by someone who recognized my critical thinking skills and began introducing me to the ways of corporations—how they are run, what sort of data is needed to ensure their success, how to navigate big projects, and more. This person remains a mentor to this day. (And she still pushes me to greater excellence.)

I started to discover, though, very early on that not everyone has critical thinking skills—or knows how to use the results of their thinking or analysis if they have them. This realization was powerful— because critical thinking is my superpower.

Get off the Hamster Wheel

If you haven't realized by now, I am the swipe-left boss. So far, I have used that analogy as it applies to noise and distractions. However, it's also about hopping off the hamster wheel. Without time to think, without the "space" in your mind and home or office to think, you will just spin and spin—and get nowhere.

Once again, my accident reminded me so clearly why this is important. In some ways it forced me to stop and think. Here's what someone in chronic pain must do—mental calculations in our head: *If I do this extra work all week with my team to meet our sales quota, then I will be unable to socialize or do anything extra on the weekend, which will be my time to think and rest. If I do too many errands and "extra," I will end up using all my energy for things that do not fit with my stated goals.* Chronic pain patients must constantly weigh the efforts of one thing or another and the energy that will take against what they absolutely *need* to get done. Hence, we swipe left on the stuff that doesn't really matter.

Now while I will be the first to tell you that I am a person who cuts through the noise and nonsense, my accident took my ability to make any other choice away from me. Weekends became my time to regroup and strategize and critically think, so much so that my husband will tease me that within twenty minutes of every movie that we start, we have to rewind and start it again because I'm working on my blog or crunching numbers. It's my time to plan my days and weeks and to see the big picture of it all.

It's funny too because my husband and I have a rule: three days apart is our limit. We really try to honor that. However, I do appreciate a weekend to myself once in a while. Why? It's my time to critically think in silence—no TV, no "noise." It's just my dog and me on the couch and my magical device (my phone!). Even when he is here, he knows that when I'm in that thinking space and everything's quiet, that is my time to be still and not move and to get in that zone I talked about in Roar of the Beast mode. Roar of the Beast does not mean "go, go, go" on the hamster wheel, just being a human machine. Roar of the Beast is a mindset.

The Steps of Critical Thinking

So are you on the hamster wheel, or are you a critical thinker? Do you think going a million miles an hour means you are working harder than everyone else? If so, what about working *smarter*?

You can train yourself to be a critical thinker. There are specific steps that are part of the process. One of the most important things before you start, though, is to *not* have an answer in mind ahead of time. Don't preguess the answers. You want to be as objective as possible. If you're not, forget about the exercise completely.

1. *What's your question?* The first step is to identify what problem you are trying to solve so you know where and what sources you should seek for information. Your question can be big and open ended, but for the best results of critical thinking, be precise so that the information you gather is specific to your query.

2. *Gather your data.*

   - This could be sales figures. It could also be the results of customer surveys. It could be industry figures and trends.

   - You need to wed your question to the data—gathering extra data that does not pertain to your issue isn't helpful and just confuses matters.

3. *Analyze and evaluate the data.* Analyzing the data is more than just looking at a bunch of numbers and plugging them into a formula.

   - For example, maybe there are two or three popular schools of thought about the trends in your industry. When you analyze the data, you would also be looking for bias, looking at how reliable your sources are, etc.

- Another example is you might have a lot of data pre-COVID. That data may not reflect anything about the current market, supply chain, and so on—and may simply be outdated. You will also want to be sure the data reflects your customers. Make sure the data is relevant.

- Have you ever seen a health study touted on a website saying something like, "This new drug cures diabetes in 80 percent of the people who tried it." But then when you read the fine print or more in depth, you discover this so-called study was of twelve people. Data is only as good as its reliability and relevance.

4. *Weigh your opinion or decision.* Now it's time to objectively examine all the information you have and make a decision based on facts. We're often taught to trust our gut or instincts. In detective stories the cop may have a hunch. It is wonderful to have a strong inner voice. However, with critical thinking, it's essential to back up your decision with the facts at your disposal.

5. *Determine your action steps.* Now that you have a decision, what are you going to do about it?

Increasing your critical thinking skills is an essential part of the Get It Together mindset. You are most definitely not "together" if you are putting out fires without actionable steps, a plan, and big-picture thinking.

Big Picture Versus "It's All in the Details"

Big-picture thinking is an important part of critical thinking. This thinking looks at the decisions you are making and considers their impact on your life or on your team, division, or company as a whole.

The big picture includes your intrinsic motivations and goals. For example, every single one of us has had a week (or month) where our job is a grind. I know, for example, that when companies assemble their annual report, the team, as the deadline approaches, will be proofing and reproofing every number repeatedly—there is simply no room for mistakes. It's tedious work. But then the push at the end is long, grinding hours too. For me, every time I've been part of an acquisition, those months around the deal are brutal in terms of hours everyone puts in. I remember once working until two in the morning and getting up at six for two weeks straight.

A big-picture thinker can look at times when it's a real grind, where grit is needed, and see the big goal—both personal and corporate. This look at the value and reason for the temporarily brutal times allows the person to see that it's not forever. It's for now. (And we'll talk about this in chapter 8, "Working through the Pain.") But it's all in the service of the big idea or goal.

Critical thinking *also* includes the details. The detailed plan, though, has to be just that—a plan. (And we'll talk more about this too!) There is a danger in getting caught up in the minutiae without a plan. That's when you see micromanagement. As a leader, you want your team to provide details and data—but to motivate them, you should be very clear how that data and those details fit into the company's larger purpose and vision.

What Do *You* Think?

I have championed and wanted to grow every single person I have ever hired. Even the rare times when someone turned out not to be a fit for their position, I still wanted them to move on to something that *would* be a fit and would offer as much advice and help as possible.

I have had, throughout my career, several assistants—most of them women. I hired each of them because I believed in them and their talents. Once they are acclimated to their positions, I have sent them as my proxy to various meetings. One time my assistant called me and said she was very nervous. "I don't know what to say, Puja."

Now this was simply untrue. (And sometimes people need to be confronted with facts.) I had given her all the tools to succeed. (I would never send someone into a meeting to wing it without being prepared.) I had even given her an outline of how to do the presentation. I tried to remember my first presentation all those years ago to the CFO. It can be nerve-racking—but preparation and critical thinking are what get you through.

This is the pep talk I gave her: "Listen, I need you to get off this phone, and I need you to do some critical thinking about what you should say based on our discussion and the data. And then you can do it." And she did, just like I knew she could.

One of my past assistants went successfully into sales. Another is my chief of staff. I will always promote those who get it together. But it's not just my assistants or people starting out in their sales careers but even my leaders will also ask, "What do you think I should do?"

My response is always, "What do *you* think you should do?" It's that ability to critically think that many people do not have or don't cultivate enough.

Carving Out the Think Time

More than once I have heard someone say, "If you want to know what you value, look at your bank statement." What does that mean? Well, if you say you value philanthropy or giving to charity but your bank statement doesn't show any giving, then are you really living your value? If you say you value self-improvement but you don't show any expenses toward a gym or a class to learn something new (whether that's personal, like a watercolor class, or professional, like a certification), do you really value that?

The same can be said for critical thinking. I already told you earlier that I tell my people to take a Think Day once a month. I value critical thinking—and I show it by making sure my team carves out think time. You cannot say you value critical thinking and then look at your Outlook or Google Calendar and see it's so jam-packed that there's no time to eat a snack, let alone spend time thinking of strategy (which is essentially business's "big picture" thinking).

Let me give you an example. I was asked by my CEO to start a brand-new sales division for my company. This was new logo acquisition, which means building a new sales division that can sell to brand-new clients quickly. It can sound so simple when you write it in a single sentence; however, to no one's surprise, this involved a *lot* of data analysis, pricing, and packaging, not to mention a brand-new group of sellers and leaders—whose thinking I was tasked to transform.

This is what thinking time looks like for me: I wake up every morning and have an hour just for me. At that hour it's quiet, the neighborhood is still, there's no noise. I typically take in two or three quick financial news bites and then look at what the stock market's likely going to do that day based on the Asian markets (time difference) and what's going on in various sectors. I have my coffee. Then in the stillness and the peace, I consider not only the data but also the strategy. What data am I going to need, and will that data tell me if the strategy I am considering is correct or not?

I look at low and high sales—and at the median. I look at customer type (media, entertainment, brand agency?). I look at the number of users, and I want to see if this hypothesis that I have in my brain is actually right. Note that, using our steps in critical thinking, I have not already decided my path—I have a hypothesis, but I want to look at it objectively.

There are some people who latch on to a hypothesis—and then look for the data to support it. That defeats the purpose of a hypothesis. Don't be too attached to your idea until you know it is backed up by supportive data. You don't want to be spitballing things against a wall. Too many sales leaders charge forward without evidence. I critically think, and I feel good about it based on my experiences, but I want the data to support it.

Now the funny thing is I recently took a sabbatical, and writing this book was part of that time. I actually did not have to wake up super early during those months. However, that think time is part of my peace of mind. The morning is very important to me. It allows me to set my stage for the day, for the week, for what I'm thinking about. I write down my thoughts in my phone—which is like an appendage for me. I don't take action right away. I usually want to mull on it a little bit more. That's my way of critical thinking.

WHERE'S YOUR HOUR? PERMISSION GRANTED

Remember when I said that sometimes it seems like people need "permission" because they have a hard time giving it to themselves? I hold my people accountable for their hour of thinking time. Why do I insist on it?

Unfortunately, we live in a world where we are so wired 24/7, and people are so stressed out by all the demands on their time that they feel like they cannot find that hour. I think this is especially true for women (though there are plenty of men who feel this way).

Trust me, if you want to be a better leader, mom, grandma, partner, husband, friend, salesperson, or anything, you need that hour. If you can't find it—if you literally look at your schedule and cannot find a window of time for yourself to think—you have not learned the word *no*.

Now to be fair, there are single parents, people whose jobs do not value work-life balance, and people with very pressing issues—such as caring for elderly parents while also raising kids or going through difficult personal circumstances. It is a deep flaw of some so-called self-help or empowerment books when it's oversimplified.

This is when I remind people that "it's for now, not forever." In other words perhaps there is a very real reason why the hour is near impossible to find right now. But it should be a goal you are moving toward. To that end, look at that schedule and see if there are some time slots that are given over to commitments you don't even care about.

Here's an example. I have a friend who, when her first child was born and eventually entered school, was the class mom, who then grew to organizing a half dozen PTA breakfasts each school year, and she also took on the role of leader of her daughter's Brownie troop and, it seemed, a half dozen other responsibilities. But when we were discussing this insane schedule of hers, I had to stop her. "Do you love doing all this? *Love* it?"

"I love being a class mom, but really, I was guilted into the PTA stuff. And I hate Brownies—some of the girls are so poorly behaved I spend the whole time yelling for them to calm down." While this is one specific example, I know for a fact that countless parents get roped into similar situations.

No—two letters. You can say no, and it's OK. You need to find that hour—and examine that overloaded schedule of yours for a place where that hour is hiding in a maelstrom of activities.

My mother often tells me that my husband and I need to socialize more. No, we don't. We keep the people who are dear to us close, but we also know that we have a plan (which I will discuss in a later chapter) and goals—and saying no in this overscheduled society is the only way we're going to achieve all we aspire to.

Leadership and Critical Thinking

As a leader, I want my team to be critical thinkers. I help them as individuals. But I also help them as a team, even if they sometimes don't know it at first.

When I started at my CRO position, I wanted my new teams to do a QBR. I gave them the format, and I sent it to them, and that was all that I gave them. I got over a hundred Slack messages, and I didn't respond to any of them. The next day came, and they were looking pretty darn irritated. They hated me. I acted innocent and said, "What? Let's talk about what you all have here."

I had one leader who felt like he could say anything, which I really appreciate. "Puja," he said in front of everyone, "this was rough."

I nodded. "It was supposed to be. Why was it rough?"

"Well, some of the stuff, we ... really didn't know what you were asking for. So we actually had to think about it. We had to all talk to one another—try to figure it out."

"Wait ... what? What is this miraculousness that's happening right now?"

The team members each kind of chuckled. So he went on, "It was still hard, even *with* us all helping one another."

I nodded. "It was meant to be hard. It was meant to make you think. And frankly it was meant for all of you to work together as a team. All of you came from different parts of the organization. We are now under one umbrella called Go to Market. And if you all are kind of mad, even if it's at my expense, thinking, 'That Puja sucks. This task sucks,' guess what? I don't care because you all had the first lesson in working as a team, number one. And you got your second individual lessons about critical thinking."

Of course, I was able to make them laugh, and by the end of the meeting, there was some (slightly begrudging) appreciation for what the whole process taught them.

People who can think critically do.

However, it went way beyond preparing a particular quarterly report because I want every single member of my team to get ahead—and people who can think critically do.

Now I don't want you to think I'm not sharing any of my own early experiences—I didn't learn how to lead this way by accident. I have had a mentor since my first corporate job. She was my manager—out of twenty-five—and I was nineteen. We would go out for happy hour on Friday nights, and in my nineteen-year-old mind, the workweek ended as soon as we walked out the door on Friday. But she used to tell me, "I'll pick you up tomorrow morning at nine." A Saturday? What fresh madness was this?

She would show up at my parents' house, pick me up, and take me for breakfast to Burger King, and we'd head to the office and deal with pricing sheets and sales and price points. In the quiet of an empty corporate office, we'd stay for about five or six hours, and it was a whole new education. I learned how to do analysis—how to make the numbers dance. I learned not only how to use data but also what data to ask for in the first place. I began to understand medians and outliers and how to interpret graphs. Essentially, those Saturdays helped train me to critically think.

When I turned twenty-two, I began working full-time, and I went to work for the head of strategy. I knew how to look at this type of data. Julie had taught me all she knew. I could look at financial data, sales data, and product data. And so when I went for my first presentation, I wasn't even nervous. It was as if I had learned a whole new language.

A woman I know took many years of French in high school and college. Then she spent an entire summer in Paris and then the French countryside, courtesy of her college graduation gift. By the end of the summer, after using her language skills, she began dreaming in French. That was the moment, she said, that she knew she was truly fluent. For me it was much the same. What I learned with that skill set stayed with me. I still will often eat dinner and then boot up my laptop to again dive into data (something we will *really* discuss in detail in our next chapter on the winning formula).

Most of us do not stay at the same company from the time we enter our professional careers on to retirement. Critical thinking skills, however, follow you from position to position. You've learned the language of critical thinking and analysis—and now you can "speak" it and dream it, and you'll never lose that talent. Look, you really are getting it together!

STRAIGHT TALK
FROM PUJA

In this chapter you have some real homework. But I promise it's going to build on everything you've done so far—and set you up for success going forward.

1. The first critical question you should be thinking about is, what does your schedule look like this week? Go. Open your electronic calendar. What does it look like? I am going to tell you right now, just like I tell my coaching clients, that if it's a schedule with no time to even make and eat a sandwich, you're setting yourself up for failure. Working to exhaustion without a plan—just moving, moving, doing, doing without time to critically think—may make you a temporary star. But it won't make you a superstar in the long run.

2. Relentless elimination—that's your next step. *Where is your hour?* That's right, where is it? Get specific. If you can't find your thinking hour, you have a real issue. The solution, then, is *relentless elimination.* What can you take out of your life so that you find your hour? For every single meeting or appointment, ask yourself, "Do I really need to be there? Really?"

3. Critically think about the plans you've been making in the book so far. What's working? What's not working? How many "green" highlights do you have for goals and tasks completed? How many red?

4. What's standing in your way? For example, and I'm going to be frank, if you are trying to have career success and your personal life is a mess—your kids don't have bedtimes, your partner doesn't do their fair share around the house, you're partying too hard, you can't recall the last time you had twenty-four hours to yourself, you eat like crap, and you never exercise or take time to do some self-care—that's a

problem. If you've identified a problem, how are you going to fix it?

5. Identify *one* thing you are going to cut out from your life to find your hour. Now cut it—without guilt. If you have to, practice in front of the mirror. Better yet, develop some ready responses to avoid overcommitting. These might include "That doesn't work for me this week" or "That isn't something I'm willing to commit to right now" or "No" or "Thanks for asking, but I'm not available. "

GET IT
TOGETHER

CHAPTER 6

The Winning Formula

Winning is the most important thing in my life,
after breathing. Breathing first, winning next.

—GEORGE STEINBRENNER

People change, the market changes, the types of people you're leading change, new technologies come out. But the formula for success in sales and business is the same.

Don't be fooled into thinking, "It can't be the same; it can't be that easy." I know, if it was that easy, everybody would be doing it. But then again, as we saw in the last chapter, not everyone knows how to think critically.

Let's return to the figure we had in chapter 3. Remember that the roof of the house was "revenue growth." That is the goal. It's what we're striving for. The foundation of the house is your people/teams. The four pillars are

1. the data;

2. the competition;

3. addressable market; and

4. identifying the breaks.

Foundation: Your People

There is a famous African proverb that a fabulous mentor once told me: "If you want to go fast, go alone. If you want to go far, go together." That is apropos of this section. The foundation of every house is what is needed to hold the building steady. In the winning formula, this is your people.

Understanding the talent that you have in place and analyzing their assets—who has what gifts, what needs to be developed—is essential. From there, you need to figure out what to subsequently do to adjust your levels upward—the foundation of the formula for success.

Any time you take over a team, you are not starting it from scratch. You "inherit" people. Even if you are building a new team or division, you're still inheriting existing people. Thus, the first step always begins with a talent assessment—determining if you have the right people for your goals and if they are the right fit.

I'll give you an example. I inherited a VP of sales—a gentleman who seemed particularly ill suited to that role. It was an open secret; however, none of the higher-ups in the organization—as in absolutely zero—had given him any of this feedback or had helped coach him along the way. And so pretty much, they told me my job was to get rid of him (or to make the sales division run well—which was basically going to mean the same thing). However, I wanted to assess him for sixty days—thinking that, with the right kind of direction, perhaps the DEFCON solution would not be necessary.

What I noticed was that this VP was not a leader—in fact, he had his assistant leading all his sales meetings. That was a telltale sign something was not right. I asked him for a proper forecast—he didn't seem to know how to do that.

I also noticed something else. One of the enterprise leaders was a superstar. I knew right away he was going to be ready for a much bigger role. He didn't know it yet, but he was!

After my sixty-day assessment, I let the VP of sales go. Quite frankly the proverbial you-know-what hit the fan. It seemed some of the people around me (and above me) were upset that I had done the hard thing, the difficult thing no one enjoys.

But what's interesting is the minute he left, I could actually do my job. I was being hindered in things like forecasting meetings and other planning because he was not capable of providing me with the information we *all* needed to be successful. So a big lesson here is that when you evaluate the team, you have to trust your initial gut sense. Regardless of what anyone's told you—good, bad, or ugly—you have to trust your gut because if you don't, you can potentially carry someone on your team who not only is ill suited for their position but also can drag down the rest of the team around them.

If you don't make decisions quickly and swiftly, it will only be to your demise. The number one problem that I see with new leaders is that they are not willing to make the hard decisions. The difficult decisions are the most important decisions you will ever make when it comes to people.

Now I am going to tell you a true story of how not making the hard decisions can harm you. I typically have this sixth sense about people. So I once inherited a team that I called the Bad News Bears.

They were at the very bottom—which meant when I inherited them, I was at the bottom too.

There was a guy on the team I'll call Freddie. My gut was telling me he was a problem on the team, but I wanted time to observe. I laid out what the plan and structure were going to be. Sitting in my office, he applauded them and assured me he would follow them. He even seemed excited.

What I didn't know was that, in my *office*, he supported the ideas and plan I had. But he was only half following them. The first month everyone was getting used to the new system. The second month Freddie hit his number. I thought, "Yes! I can turn this guy around." But by the third month, he went back to his normal self, distracting the floor, being incredibly negative and definitely not a team player or on board with what I was trying to do.

Well, I hadn't yet learned. I allowed him to continue for four months. In those months I kept trying to pull him up from where he was and get him fully up to speed. That means for four months I lost the trust of my team. Everybody knew what he was doing. It took me too long to make the hard decision. So for four months, I not only lost the trust of my team but I also then needed to hire someone new and train them, and it would be another four months or so until we were fully up and running. Right then and there, we lost over half a year.

The big lesson is that the foundation of your team is your people and your ability to assess them—and assess them quickly—and promote the ones that are doing well. Promote them because they're going to be like pinch hitters for the team. In the meantime, in baseball parlance, trade or cut the team members who cannot perform.

I'll also continue my baseball analogy. You can take someone from a B+ player to an A player—from the Triple-As to the majors—if they have the talent and are trainable *and* willing to work hard. But it's very unlikely to take someone from a rookie league straight to the majors—especially if the talent and hard work is not there. In fact, that would be nearly impossible. Transforming a C player to a B player is actually a lot harder than taking a B+ player to A. In the meantime, if this is your sales team, that weak, lazy player is going to suck the life out of the entire team.

Sometimes you may have a solid team member in terms of work ethic, but they are simply not matched to the job. Not everyone is cut out for sales. One man worked for me on the first team I ever led. You have never seen someone so capable at analyzing data and putting it into bright, shiny reports with figures with lots of numbers after the decimal points. He was so exact and so talented at numbers. But sales? Not so much. Finally, after observing him and having four one-on-ones with him, I was frank. "I am not sure this position is a fit for you. But where I do think you excel is at financials. I know this is strange for a manager to tell you, but I sincerely think you need to go back to school and get a degree in accounting." I told him, "I think I'm a genius with numbers, but you understand numbers better than I do on a whole other level."

Three weeks later he told me he had applied to another company. I wished him luck and told him to stay in touch. Two years later I heard from him on LinkedIn. He had become an accountant and was working for one of the Big Four firms. His message was, "I just wanted to let you know that was the best thing you ever did for me. It sucked at the time, but it was a gift. This is what I was meant to do. I'm very happy."

So that goes really to the people part. Your direct reports are your keys to the kingdom. If you don't have the right direct reports, whether that's salespeople, HR people, sales leaders, or finance people, you're going to be dead in the water. Often, in the first ninety days of taking over a leadership position, people run around like a chicken with their head cut off and meet with this one and that one. But you need to spend the most time with your direct reports. They also frankly need to assess you. They are thinking, "Can I work with this person or not?"

I also like to give my people forecasting assignments and let them do the job of critical thinking and see what they come up with. Once I see where everyone is starting from, then I can start my lessons.

So that is a foundation of every team, period, end of story. If you have the right ones, you are in decent shape. If you've had to move some of them out, you're rehiring.

The last part of the people aspect is you also have to meet with the stakeholders who are going to help make your job easier. During this early period, for most leaders, those stakeholders will be finance and human resources. Those are your two besties. They will be your besties forever. This is important. I think too many new leaders forget about meeting with their stakeholders. They're so worried about meeting with the boss, with their customers, and with other people. And none of that really matters in the beginning. You have to meet with the people who are going to help you put together the financial plan, help you with the comp plan, help you if you have to hire and fire, and understand what the product road map is. If you don't meet with your stakeholders, you're also dead in the water because you're not really extending an olive branch to the people whose job, whether they know it or not, is to help revenue grow.

Pillar 1: The Data

W. Edwards Deming, the famous engineer and management consultant, famously said, "In God we trust. All others must bring data."

So this is typically what happens at every organization:

Saying number one is "My data's bad. I can't really trust it."

Saying number two is "We don't have enough data."

Saying number three is "We have too much data. I don't know what to do with it."

For me as a revenue leader, there are certain pieces of data that I need to obtain. The answer to any of those three statements is … tough. You have to figure out a way to get *your* data. So whether that's through a sales operations person or you have a data team at the company (increasingly common), you have to figure out how to get it. Now the key is what questions you ask to get the data that you need. So for me, number one—period, end of story—is retention and renewal rates.

Let me explain to you why. If you are selling to a ton of customers but your retention rate is 70 percent, you're doomed. That means you have a product problem. That means you have a sales rep problem, maybe a customer success and support problem. That means your salespeople don't passionately care about and pursue renewals. To help you with your retention and renewal, you really have to start understanding your current customer base—because your current customers will tell you a lot about what the future is going to look like.

Next, you must slice and dice your data. What does that mean? I begin consolidating industries and sectors into pods. So for example, you are not going to have categories such as semiconductor firms and then also manufacturing firms. Instead, they should all go into one pod called skilled labor. That information is like pure money to me.

Number two is new customer data. How many new customers are you acquiring per month? Utilize the same filters, such as industry, employee size, or other factors you want to cluster together. In this way you can understand who's really buying your product and who's not, and then you dig further so you can understand why they're not buying and figure out if it makes sense to pursue them. Ideally you would like the data to cover a two- to three-year window. With a longer window, you can spot trends. While looking at the last six months is fine, you really want to look at a longer window if you can.

E-commerce data is also priceless. At companies in the past, that data helped me see what were enterprise accounts and what were midmarket.

Now I'm going to pause here and say that, on occasion, someone remarks to me that they think I want too much data—and that I am not a strategist. Well, after I finish laughing about this, I can respond that yes, I *am* a strategic thinker, but data helps me reach my decision on what the strategy is going to be. I am not going to randomly come up with a plan, pulling something out of the air like, "We should expand internationally." Should we? I don't know—let's see what the data says.

If you are any type of P&L leader, you also want to look at the last two years of historical financials because if you don't, you have no idea where you were. You have no idea what the anomalies are. You have no idea of cyclicality in the business. As an example, in November and December, our retail business falls off the hill. Now that we know that we've had two years of that, we can strategize how to combat it. But if you don't look at those financials, you're not even going to know what you're walking into. You're not going to understand that June or July or January is the month where you need to be proactive, not reactive.

Pillar 2: The Competition

Ray Kroc once said, "Competition can try to steal my plans and copy my style. But they can't read my mind; so I'll leave them a mile and a half behind." Yes, we're at our next pillar—competition.

I can remember coming aboard my CRO position and asking who our competition was. I would ask this in every one-on-one, and I wrote the answers down on sticky notes. (Confession: I am a Post-it addict.) I slapped them up on the wall, and before I knew it, there were fifty competitors up there.

That won't work. You can't really compete with fifty all at once. It's the same logic I gave you about holding yourself to three goals at a time instead of a hundred. So next, I at least needed to understand our top three, maybe the top five—not just understand but also know them inside and out. Here again, when I talk about getting to know your stakeholders and building relationships with them, my marketing stakeholder came in extraordinarily handy here.

I asked him to design an internal survey. We needed to get that list of fifty down to numbers one, two, and three. We could then do a deep dive into pricing structures and what they offered versus what we did. Now data is not simply my sticky notes. It's more than a list.

This is where asking the right questions makes a difference. What I *really* want to know is, if one of my reps loses to a competitor, at what price point do we lose?

I love a white paper as much as the next gal—but what I really want is a *combat paper*. Here's how to combat Competitor A, here's how to combat Competitor B, and here's the game plan for Competitor C. Your salespeople—whatever the industry—are going to run into your top competitors over and over. You need to be prepared. We have one sheet for each with rebuttals for every single area.

I'll be real here. Yes, we all compete against ourselves. We compete against our internal doubts and insecurities. But in the business world, if you don't have a combat plan, you're going to lose on the battlefield.

Pillar 3: Addressable Market

The definition of *addressable market* is the total revenue opportunity (or total demand) for a given set of products or services inside your market today. It's often abbreviated as TAM (total addressable market).

To give you a real-life example, at one company there was chatter about selling to the international market. However, the *data* demonstrated that 99 percent (!) of our sales occurred in North America. Thus, it made sense to continue our focus on North America. Now it's important to know that any decisions along these lines are for now—not forever. Long-range strategy might include pursuing the international market. But in the here and now, we had not fully penetrated North America—and it was fertile ground.

Our next step was to figure out what markets we would expand into. Marketing, once again, is a bestie. They can help you figure out your TAM—and also your serviceable addressable market (SAM). The SAM is the portion of your market that aligns with your business model and takes into account your geographical limitations. For us the focus was North America.

The next part, which is what a consulting firm did for us, was analyze which portion of the market we could realistically capture based on XYZ constraints in the market. The number they came up with was a billion dollars, with a *b*. We were, at that point, under $25 million. So we should just go out there and sell and get that billion, right? Wrong.

How many sales reps do you have? What's their capacity? How many customers can you service? Can you maintain your overall retention and renewal rates?

You have to have the internal structure to support your ambitions. So we settled on $50 million for the next year. I felt we could reasonably double our sales without sacrificing service.

You have to have the internal structure to support your ambitions.

My rule is you set the number in your head, your people's number, and you build quotas on 10 percent higher than that. So we *actually* set our number at $55 million. Remember, this is not a number I pulled out of a hat. It is based on all the analysis, all those one-on-ones, all that market research, all that forecasting.

Pillar 4: Identifying the Breaks

Our last pillar is identifying the breaks in the machine—but there are two parts to this. One is head count. But anyone in business knows that head count doesn't grow on trees—so again, data, data, data. Next, you've gone to the board with your number (which is always 10 percent higher—don't forget that). After the first thirty days, you look at your data again. What worked? What didn't?

Now here's another tip from Puja. Thirty days is not too soon to look. Everyone thinks it's too soon (not the people who work for me). They'll say you need to give it ninety days. No, you don't.

Here's an example. I had someone working for me who was as big a data nerd as I am—shocking, I know. We pulled information from Salesforce and from this source and that one. I wanted to look after thirty days.

What can thirty days tell you? It can tell you if there's a break in your system. This woman pulled all the data, and we saw a problem right away. There wasn't enough activity happening—and sales is really a formula. And part of that formula is based on activity.

Now that your thirty-day check-in has revealed a problem, what's your combat plan? I met with my leaders, and I revamped their one-on-one sheets. Then I told them, since everything's electronic, that I wanted to be tagged on all their people's sheets. That is not punitive—and I reassure them I'm on their side. I told them each something along the lines of "I know you think that I'm micromanaging you. I'm not. I'm giving you a formula for success. It is *not* a critique. We're all succeeding together. I need to understand what is happening, and I can't ever understand what is happening until I see it."

By the second month, we started to see an uptick not just in sales but also in activity, such as sequencing through outreach, phone calls, etc. At the end of the second month, we could now look at individual trends. Who and where needed fixing? Remember when I mentioned that our renewal rate was 70 percent? We set a goal for 90 percent of *on-time* renewal because renewals are great, but if they're late, people are not going to consider "back pay" for those late months. That's flushing money down the giant corporate toilet.

Applying the Four Pillars to Your Everyday Life (Yes, the One Outside Work)

Just one last note: while I have offered a formula for success in business based on my experiences, believe it or not, many of these principles can be applied to your everyday life—the one out there, not at the office. How? Let's just use one simple example that so many of us relate to.

You want to lose twenty pounds. Well, first things first, who are your people? What's the foundation? Do you have a walking buddy? Maybe your partner is willing to eat healthily along with you.

Now you need to gather your data. And no, I don't mean just what the number on the scale is. Instead, look at your trends. Do you always gain weight at the holiday time?

By analyzing what you want to accomplish against what the numbers will actually tell you, you can come up with a plan.

Has your weight crept up five pounds a year for the last four years? By analyzing what you want to accomplish against what the numbers will actually tell you, you can come up with a plan.

Your addressable market? What activities do you need to generate to attack your problem?

Your breaks? Where are your weaknesses? For many people, they eat when bored or stressed. When you know where your personal breaks are, you can come up with a combat plan.

The bottom line is when you start to think in terms of data *and* solutions and strategies, you can start to see patterns and trends elsewhere in your life—and make changes to win at both your career and life.

STRAIGHT TALK
FROM PUJA

This chapter's Straight Talk is about applying this to your career. If you want to get it together, then learning how to approach your work dilemmas with the mindset of the four pillars will be your secret formula. (All right, I suppose it's not so secret if I am sharing it with everyone—but your own story and activities will make it unique.)

Choose a problem or an aspiration. So it could be that your sales are flat. Or it could be they are "OK," but you have an ambitious goal for this year. Now sit down and write out the elements of the four pillars.

1. Data: What data do you need? Who do you need to gather it from? What trends does the data tell you? What does the data tell you historically?

2. Competition: Who is your competition? Not the hundred other companies in your space. Who are your top three competitors? How are you going to compete against them? What are their weaknesses? What are yours?

3. Addressable market: Define this for your product or service.

4. Breaks in the machine: Now is the time to analyze where your breaks are—so you can fix them. Are *you* the weak link? Is there something holding you back that you need to address?

Once you have completed this exercise, what is the biggest thing you learned from this analysis? Were there any surprises?

CHAPTER 7

Stick to Your Strategy: When the Going Gets Tough, the Tough Stick with It

Without strategy, execution is aimless.
Without execution, strategy is useless.

—MORRIS CHANG

I'm so proud of you. By now you are getting it together in all areas of your life, right? You've written out your quarterly goals. You're swiping left. You are shutting out distractions.

So why is it still so hard? Well, if you are doing your goals correctly, it's because they are a reach. If you are making changes in your personal life, say, in how you run your household, there are growing pains. Thus, this chapter is about sticking to your strategy.

Change Takes Time

I don't know about you, but I am terribly impatient. My life moves at a million miles an hour when I'm all in on a project. I want the data I asked for yesterday. I want the remodel of my kitchen done two weeks ago. (All right, *anyone* who has ever remodeled their kitchen wants to jump out the kitchen window—even if it's on the first floor.) I want the "new me" to be here in a shiny bow, achieving everything she sets her mind to. But I know life doesn't work like that.

Let's start with some science and some myth. For years many of the self-help gurus out there would tout that if you would just get rid of a bad habit by trying something new and creating a new habit, in about twenty-eight days, the hard work would be over. So for example, they might tell you that since you want to lose weight and get fit, if you lace up those sneakers first thing in the morning for three or four weeks—voila!—you will be a fitness buff.

These kinds of habits could even be deeper and more difficult, such as giving up alcohol (I've done it to keep myself sharp) or cigarettes or arguing with your mom. Unfortunately, for most people, the bad habits or the nonhabits (i.e., *not* exercising) usually have a pretty firm grip on your life. My friend's mother started smoking when she was thirteen. I have had friends who struggled with alcohol who say they realized they had a problem for *years*. And I know plenty of people with the best of intentions who will say, "I'm not going to engage when my mom/dad/partner/sister/friend says *x*, *y*, and *z* to bait me or to start something." And then there we are, arguing.

If it makes you feel any better, those self-help gurus were wrong. (Doesn't that make you feel better? See, it wasn't you!) According to a study in the *European Journal of Social Psychology*, it takes 18 to 254 days to make a positive change and a new behavior. The average is 66 days.[18]

I am *thrilled* you bought this book. (Really! Make sure you write me at my website pujarios.com to tell me how the Get It Together program is working for you.) However, it cannot be a book that sits on your nightstand with no action on your part or is stored on your Kindle or phone to glance at once in a while. No, to make real change to get it together, you have to do the work. And that is hard, and there's no getting around it. But would you really, *really* want something that came too easily?

My Real Story of Sticking to My Strategy: A Play in Three Acts

ACT I: IT STARTED WITH $3

I am going to be really vulnerable here and tell you my honest, swear-to-you, true story of my strategy and sticking with it. My story starts in my twenties. I had taken a break from the corporate world and found myself the GM of several high-end nightclubs.

I had met my husband, and I told him we both needed to work on our goals—each of us separately yet together. I had my goals in the industry I was in. He was a writer and also in the music industry, where he was a legend. Like many twentysomethings, we were burning the candle at both ends, and we both worked in very demanding professions that took up a lot of our time. But we had dreams, and we were going for them.

---

18   "How Long Does It Take to Form a Habit?" Healthline, accessed January 1, 2023, https://www.healthline.com/health/how-long-does-it-take-to-form-a-habit#base-figure.

In total maybe eighteen months went by, and I became very disenchanted with the way my employer was handling some issues. I had some ethical concerns, among other things, so I quit—without a backup plan. (Don't do what Puja did, kids.)

I went to Bear's (my name for my husband) house, and Bear wasn't working full-time at that time either. Between the two of us, we had three dollars to our name.

Pain is what brought me to my success ultimately.

My sister was living with me at the time, and she had a good job. Thank goodness because she was paying our living expenses.

This was in late spring, and Bear and I went to Riis Park (in Chicago) in the early evening. The sky was a soft gray, and we set down a blanket and did some stargazing (a free activity). Then I said, "I don't want to have three dollars in my pocket anymore."

We will get to this a little more in our next chapter on working through the pain, but pain is what brought me to my success ultimately. I was in enough pain about our circumstances that I knew we needed to make real and profound change. We needed to get it together.

> Be patient and tough; someday this
> pain will be useful to you.
>
> —OVID

He felt the same—which is one of the amazing things. We were two people who met at a time when we *both* wanted to grow and change and develop a strategy to do so. Sometimes ambition etc. can be scary in a partnership if both people are not on the same page.

I said to him, "Well, we are going to figure this out. We have to set goals. We're gonna have to hit them and go for them—hard. I want a penthouse with a rooftop garden, and I want a Mercedes-Benz. We're going to have to work for what we want." And he agreed.

Now I will tell you, money is a motivator for most, if not all, of us. But for me, articulating those dreams was really about visualizing the dream—the goal. Money, ultimately, if you are successful, is a way to do nice things for the people in your life, a way to enjoy the fruits of your labor, a way to see the world or to live in a place you've always wanted to live.

We started with three dollars—I am not kidding when I say that. The funniest thing was there was this ice cream cart that kept walking by us with these mango ice cream treats. They were precisely three dollars, so to "celebrate" our new mindset, we bought one to share. The ice cream man handed me our ice cream on a cone and walked off with his cart. Then the mango ice cream fell off the cone. And I thought, "This is not how this is gonna go."

ACT II: GRINDING IN SALES

Sometimes our careers take a detour. When I was in my twenties, the club business seemed exciting. I was around well-known musical acts; I had great freedom to manage the way I envisioned, but ultimately it was a brutal business I could not see staying in long term. I had many years (despite only being twenty-eight at the time) in the corporate universe, and if I really wanted to achieve those financial goals, I knew going back into that world was my path. I was good at it.

I called Xerox, and they happily (thank God) welcomed me back. They had a sales office in Chicago—and I knew that *sales* was where people made their careers. I knew I was good at sales. So it was back into that career.

Bear, meanwhile, continued with his music career. It wasn't steady, but he was (and is) amazing.

You've read enough of this book to know what I said, right? "No. We have set our goals as a couple and as individuals. If you want to pursue your passion for music, fine. But it has to be *after* your 'real' job."

He, too, entered the corporate space (but still pursued his more creative endeavors). And these were our grind years. We were like two ships passing in the night. With the hours we each worked, our only time to see each other was Saturday night and Sunday. And this was before text was so ubiquitous. And it was before Zoom. So when I say we rarely saw each other and didn't get to talk all the time, I mean it.

But I was resolute. This was what needed to be done because there was no fairy godmother who was going to sweep in with a magic wand, wave it, and give us the life we aspired to. I was driving a Honda with many miles on it. (Spoiler alert: I did eventually get that Mercedes.) We weren't even living together. But what we did have were goals that meant a lot to who each of us was.

I give him credit—he worked extremely hard at his corporate job. Then he would go home, shower, grab something to eat, and go into the studio to record his album. Rinse, repeat. See what I mean? The grind years.

These were our prime working years, and we were going to have to relentlessly execute. That's where I developed that "swipe left" mentality (even if that wasn't a thing yet). It was about removing distractions, sticking to the strategy, and staying in our lane.

At the same time, I was making some observations—noting things that I came to ultimately use in this book. For example, I saw other people with goals but no strategy. The goals were like these ideas floating by—clouds in the air you cannot grab because there's nothing solid to touch.

I had observed one of my coworkers, for example. He would come in at seven. He could have used that hour to set up himself—and our whole team—for success. Remember how much I emphasize critical thinking? He could have been utilizing that free, quiet hour before most of the team was there to figure out what our first quarter was going to look like or to think outside the box and explore new ideas.

But he never did that. Instead, he would roam the floors and frequently visit the C-level, "shaking hands and kissing babies," as they say. But he never had a strategy, never stuck to a plan.

ACT III: LEADERSHIP

My grind looks different these days. In fact, it's not a grind. It's excitement, passion, planning, leading, sharing my vision.

But I still stick to my strategies. For example, at one of the companies I worked for, an acquisition was occurring. As we all know, an acquisition is like dating. Everyone is trying to get to know everyone else—and putting on their very best face.

I also had a team to lead with a many-tens-of-millions-of-dollars goal. In the meantime, the acquisition team was demanding all sorts of data (which I understand). But in addition to that, it seemed like every day was nothing but meetings.

So I stuck to my personal policy and strategy of avoiding distractions. First, I did not reveal to my team that I had these additional stresses. *They* needed to be focused on *their* sales goals. Anything else would have been a distraction on our multimillion-dollar goal. I was not going to allow that to happen. At some point during acquisition diligence, it became a distraction for me too. I remember our one executive leadership call in particular where I had to draw a line. "If you need me here to talk about revenue, projections, future, historics, those areas in my wheelhouse, fine. Other than that, I'm not going to be in twenty meetings a day that have nothing to do with growing the business—which is our growth strategy, our plan, and needs to be executed."

At the end of the day, if our numbers weren't there when we went to close, they weren't going to buy us. I had to stick to our strategy—I had to do it for me, and I had to do it for the team. I think this is one of the number one problems with people in their strategy. They set their goals—then allow things to get in the way of them.

Let's go back to your goals. Before you set your goals, you have to define them. What is your *core* goal? Focus on that first. If you're a parent, then obviously your family and your job are both added into the mix. That's it. Everything else is a distraction.

Why Your Strategy Will Save You

I'm here to tell you (which I will share more about in the next chapter) that nothing ever goes completely smoothly, no matter how much scheduling, planning, manifesting, dreaming, or pushing you do because the truth of life is that your strategy will save you. What do I mean by that?

There will be times in life when the proverbial shit will hit the fan. There will be moments when life will throw everything at you—and I mean the bad stuff. We all know people—or have been through it ourselves—who have been bombarded by tragedies or difficult circumstances. I know someone whose husband's alcohol abuse worsened—right in time for the pandemic. The chaos and crisis that ensued nearly destroyed her. I have a friend whose family had four deaths in two years—four immediate or very close family members. In the midst of it, she was laid off because she was not performing (no wonder, given all she was going through).

The fact is none of us is spared those times in life that are very difficult. Sometimes, obviously, those times will be related to your job—layoffs or transitions in leadership that are not for the better or perhaps unreasonable comp plans or a department full of negativity. Rather than spinning around in circles, being consumed with worry, or shutting down, it is precisely your strategy that can help you through. Carl Jung once wrote, "Do the next right thing."

Doing the next right thing means looking at your strategy, at your goals, at your microsteps; determining what the next "right" thing is; and then doing it. You're not looking over there—at that thing you have no control over. You aren't looking backward. (There's a reason it's a rearview mirror—you don't look at it all the time, just a glance once in a while.) You aren't wondering what is going to happen in five years. You're just doing the next right thing.

Notice something? I did not say the next *easy* thing. Doing the next right thing isn't always easy, in fact, but focusing on it and on your strategy means you put your energy toward that one thing—not a dozen things—and take it one microstep at a time.

I'll give you another real-life example on the personal side of the equation. During the height of the COVID-19 pandemic, relationships either were strengthened or broke in half. I know a few couples who split up or considered separating. For me, COVID-19 was actually good for my well-being in some ways. I had an opportunity to reassess my career and figure out the next step for me.

When I accepted and began my new position, my boss was in New Jersey—and I was free to work from anywhere. Bear and I were still living in Chicago. And part of our long-range vision for our lives was definitely to move somewhere warmer. (I grew up for part of my childhood in Rochester, New York—it did not enamor me of the cold.)

So Bear and I took the leap. We decided to move to Miami Beach—a warm and wonderful place with a thriving music scene as well. However, for that goal to happen, we needed a strategy. I can tell you the Pentagon has nothing on us. We had this mapped out with precision. We prepared. Then we prepared some more. We had calendars—including one on the fridge so it was in our face every time we grabbed a drink or food. Every step of our strategy was mapped out.

Now just so you don't think everything went smoothly, I needed a dental crown; the two of us needed our yearly physicals because we knew we would not be set up with new doctors right away in our new city. (And as someone with fibromyalgia and rheumatoid arthritis, I especially needed to get established with a physician right away—but until then, a checkup in Chicago was in order.) Our dogs needed to be seen by the vet before we left. We had movers to schedule and boxes to pack. We had to set up new accounts in Miami at banks and arrange for our utilities to be turned off in our old city and turned on in the new one and a million other things to attend to. But our strategy made it possible. We were so committed to our schedule that we pulled it off—and didn't lose our minds or our marriage.

I will say I sincerely believe your partner can make or break your Get It Together plan. I have seen people I coach with great partnerships that help that person reach their goals. They have a strategy together—even if pursuing different careers. But I have also seen couples where one or the other is competitive, jealous, or uncomfortable with the growth their partner is going through, and they sabotage their strategy. I don't think it's done consciously. They are just not in the same space of ambition.

For Bear and me, our strategy has been in place for twenty years! Yes, you can be that disciplined for that long—with big results.

Strategy Tip: Come Out of the Gate Strong

Some things you may have to take my word on. And one of them is this: if you don't start right away with the changes you want to make to get it together and you don't execute in the first three months of the year, the rest of your year is done, end of story. That is true for your personal goals and strategy—and doubly true for business. If you don't hit your numbers in the first quarter, you're behind the eight ball the entire year. This is why the magic formula I shared in chapter 6 is *so* important. You need to set your goals ambitiously—but also with a dose of realism—to aim for numbers, sales, and progress that you can attain (not if but *when* you push yourself).

> **If you don't hit your numbers in the first quarter, you're behind the eight ball the entire year.**

I never want my people to operate like that. I never want them to operate from a state of "we're behind, we're behind, we're behind." I want them to operate from a state of "how much more can we get?" And that means my team and I come out of that gate strong—every year.

Strategy Tip: Don't Wait until You're in Trouble

I have a friend whose kid is a genius but truly struggles with ADD and anxiety. Inevitably two weeks before the end of each marking period, the house becomes a pool of chaos as all hands are on deck to try to get this kid to pass. His learning disability means he often doesn't tell his parents he's fallen behind until it's almost too late.

For Bear and me, our strategy isn't a piece of paper we take out, unfold, and look at once a quarter. It isn't something we write in a journal or appointment calendar and then shove in a desk drawer. Our strategy is a *living, breathing* program.

Each day we make adjustments. Strategy isn't etched in stone. If market conditions change, for example, your financial approach may change. If you planned to run five days a week to lose weight and get fit and you sprain your knee, your strategy may change to swimming laps.

My partner and I check in with each other on our goals daily. This means not only that we keep our strategy in mind and that we adapt and make changes as circumstances change but also that we encourage each other, lift each other, and coach each other.

Strategy Tip: Have the Difficult Conversations

When Bear and I had just three dollars to buy ice cream—and that was about it—the conversation we had was beautiful. After all, we set goals for our lives going forward and for our life together. But it was also not an easy conversation. It's wonderful to have big dreams

126

and ideas, but when you get down to strategy, how to get there, then things can be difficult.

For example, my husband wanted to *only* DJ and create music when we started our plan. But that would not get us on the same path to our goals. We fought over some of our ideas—we didn't always agree on the strategy or execution. We agreed on our *goals*—but not necessarily how to get there.

I'll give you another example. I had a coworker when we started the healthcare division at a company. She ran enterprise accounts, and I used to marvel at her intelligence. But let me tell you how her household ran. She was pregnant. She had just become a director, *and* she was going back to school to get her master's.

She and her husband had figured out how to handle their goals as individuals, a couple, and a family. He was the stay-at-home dad. (They already had one daughter.)

The conversations about that had to be detailed, honest, and tough. She knew what she wanted—and she was very willing to take on the responsibility, stress, and pressure of being the breadwinner. But her partner was also part of the strategy. He was going to take care of "everything else." If you have children, you know that's no small task.

Achieving your goals may mean hard conversations—with your kids, partner, parents, roommate, or even boss. You can't be afraid of the difficult work that goes into strategizing. That's the only way you will reach your goals.

Strategy Tip: Checks and Balances

One of the most important pieces of your strategy is knowing when you're not following your strategy. That's why you need an accountability partner (whether that is your literal partner or a friend). They provide the checks and balances to your strategy.

One of the checks/balances you need to ask them to hold you to is when you go off the path. Here's an example. Perhaps you have a goal to make ten calls a week to clients you haven't touched base with in a while. Then you have a crazy week. You don't make the calls. The next week you have too many meetings—so you skip that week. You tell yourself you will definitely do it *next* week.

Before you know it, your strategy is blown. Checks and balances will prevent you from losing your way. While we discussed taking your goals out at the end of every quarter and looking at what you accomplished—and what you didn't—and analyzing your performance, this is different. As I stated earlier in the chapter, you can't wait until you are already in trouble. Checks and balances are more frequent—just a quick check-in to see if you are wobbling.

I think that you have to do a five-minute system check every week. We do it on Sunday. And this is another swipe-left story. I sincerely feel that every single person needs time to set their plans for the upcoming workweek. Whether you wake up early on Monday morning to do it or you do it Sunday night, you can't have a strategy without that check-and-balance analysis.

We used to entertain family on weekends. Inevitably our free time was eaten up—by people we love, of course, but it still meant the same thing. It's difficult to strategize without time to consider your plans in a relaxed environment while you have time and mental space to think critically.

According to the Cambridge Dictionary, a *strategy* is "a detailed plan for achieving success in situations such as war, politics, business, industry, or sports, or the skill of planning for such situations." Checks and balances are those details. They aren't the vision—they are making sure all the little things that go into that vision are coming along.

The Inner Critic and Your Strategy

We all have an inner critic—who is usually unkind. Sometimes that inner critic is a blast from the past, that bully from childhood or a parent's criticism or a boss's or a former partner's. While the voice may sound like our own internal voice, if you listen closely, you can figure out whose voice it *really* is.

Sometimes the inner critic is *us*. We may compare ourselves with other people. (Instagram is notorious for this—everyone's lives look so picture-perfect, right down to perfect food on perfect plates in perfect kitchens.) There are those of us who look at our to-do list, or our strategy, and we can see every "failure."

When I review my strategy each Sunday, I do look at what I didn't accomplish in the previous week. But I do not beat myself up over it. Guess what? Self-criticism and harshness don't get you any closer to your big dreams. When you have a miss, it's time to figure out why, make a *new* strategy, and hit the ground running on Monday. You're always holding yourself accountable, but that doesn't mean belittling yourself.

What about when the inner critic is right? Say you had a strategy, and you didn't follow through at all. Your inner critic is giving you a hard time. Good. But the "hard time" should sound more like this: "Wow, so I didn't do any of the cold calls I said I was going to. No sense crying, 'Why? Why didn't I?' about it." Then dig deep because knowing why is the first step toward course correction.

STRAIGHT TALK
FROM PUJA

All right, let's get real with each other. Lay it on me. Are you starting to feel like you are getting it together? One of the great things about getting it together (and we'll discuss more in the final chapter) is that your life will no longer feel out of control or chaotic. It may still be beyond busy—but there's order in the chaos.

Let's look at what you should be doing (if you haven't already):

- You've set a big goal—a reach goal—in fact, two or three of them.

- You've examined that goal with hope and clarity. You hope for this big dream of yours, but you also have clarity about what it's going to take to reach it.

- You've hopped off the hamster wheel. You're still driven, but you realize you need to work smarter and with purpose, not just spinning, spinning, spinning with no forward vision.

- You've picked three (not five or six) goals for this quarter—max.

- You have practiced swiping left. If it's not helping you get to your goal, it's a distraction.

- You have not let the word *no* or a setback derail you.

- You have embraced the Roar of the Beast mode.

- You have microsteps in place as you move toward your goals.

- You embrace critical thinking.

- You have explored the four pillars and adapted the formula for your purposes.

- You have a strategy—in detail.

- You have found an accountability partner.

- You do not let weeks go by without checking in on your goals. You do it weekly and have checks and balances to "keep you honest" about how you are doing.

- You are starting to feel real change.

All right, let's just write down a few things. What are the top three strategies you are using to reach your goal? You need to come out of the gate strong. What excites you most about getting it together?

Now we're on to working through the pain.

CHAPTER 8

Working through the Pain: Failure Is Only a Lesson

Failure is not the opposite of success, it's part of success.

—ARIANNA HUFFINGTON

I deal with chronic pain. That sort of battle affects me every single day. But that's not the type of pain we're going to talk about in this chapter. Instead, we'll talk about the pain that comes from personal and career setbacks, obstacles, and stumbling blocks, from aiming for something and not reaching it and having to regroup and try again.

You know the expression "What doesn't kill you makes you stronger"? None of us enjoy failure. But failure is only a failure if you fail to learn from it.

What's Your Relationship with Failure?

Some of us are terrified of failure. (And a subset of that group are people so terrified of it that they don't even try.) Some of us are devastated by failure and are unable to regroup and get back up again. A lucky few of us have never had a really big failure. Some of us use failure as a teaching tool. Others view it as part of the pathway to ultimate success.

As someone who played sports in high school, I had my share of lost games. We can't win every single game. Every time you connect with a bat will not mean you knock it out of the park. But failure can sometimes grow bigger than we are—until it starts to look like a monster. We fear it. We might shove it under the bed where the monsters hide, but without a proper relationship with failure (where we recognize failure for what it is—not as scary as we think), that monster will keep us up late at night, staring at the ceiling in terror.

Aside from sports losses and the usual ups and downs of adolescence, my first failure was being laid off when I was in my early twenties. It was not quite a failure in the traditional sense (where you try something and fail at it); four hundred of us were laid off at once. (I guess you could say the company's leadership failed in some way.)

My work friends and I rented a party bus to take us to the unemployment office. At that point I was young—and failure was something I could view humorously, confident I would land on my feet. I was single, willing to try something new, and being laid off didn't seem like the end of the world. (Most of us feel very differently once we have dependents, mortgages, etc.)

Failure can be our teacher. It can be our motivator. It can also decimate us—if we let it. So in this chapter, let's pull that monster out from under the bed, turn on the lights, realize it's not so terrifying after all, and learn how to work through the pain.

Embrace the Suck (Again)

You may recall we discussed embracing the suck early in the book. The example I used was cold-calling. No one likes to do it, but it's something that has to get done. I try to motivate my teams by having us all do undesirable tasks like cold-calling together or gamifying it.

But this is a different "embrace the suck." Failure is not fun. ("No kidding, Puja.") You can read this entire chapter, and I can give you some mottoes and philosophy on how to handle it. But you're never going to *like* failure.

The thing about failure, though, is no one escapes life without it. Some may have more spectacular fails (Musk's Twitter implosion comes to mind) and some more modest, but failure simply is, and there is no avoiding it. *It's what you do about it that matters.*

I will never forget when one of my team members went for a promotion in another division. As I have said elsewhere, I always celebrate when my people choose to move on to pursue their passions. However, despite having gone to night school to get her MBA and having relevant experience and a fantastic personality, she was not chosen.

It's a no for now, not forever.

She came into my office, shut the door, and burst into tears. And I couldn't blame her. I can't say I've never done the same. It *hurts* to pursue something hard and not achieve it.

If that's the case, one of the first lessons I want to impart is to go ahead and embrace it. What I told her is one of my most powerful tools. "Yes, it's a no—for right now but not forever."

So many of us—particularly if we've been working hard toward something, are exhausted, or have additional stressors, family problems, etc.—can view a failure through a lens of "nothing good will ever happen again." It's like an adolescent with their very first heartache who says, "I'll never fall in love again!" (Spoiler alert: you will.) But this thinking gives the failure monster status. It makes it appear much bigger. And it may, in fact, be a *big* failure. But giving it more power just makes it worse. It's a no for now, not forever.

Don't Eat the Whole Cake

If you've ever been on a diet, sometimes we'll be so "good." A couple of pounds seem to melt away. Then we have a *big* piece of cake at our friend's birthday party. From there, we figure, "What the heck," and dive into the potato chips and dip on the buffet table—and while we're at it, we'll take a glass or two of wine. Suddenly we've fallen down a rabbit hole of breaking every single diet rule we had. And it all started with that cake.

So you had a piece of cake. That doesn't mean you go and eat the *whole* cake. Don't turn a little failure into an enormous one.

It's important that you, once again, don't make failure into the monster under the bed. Don't give it power. Put it in perspective. Your friend had a birthday party, and you enjoyed a slice of cake. Frankly, good for you!

Don't turn a little failure into an enormous one.

So let's think about this from a Get It Together standpoint. By this time you have hopefully fired up your relentless execution. Full steam ahead. You've got your microsteps. You've got your goals. Heck, you're even getting up an hour early to do thirty minutes of yoga and to spend a half hour just thinking.

But then you have a work deadline. You're so busy that you shove your goals, microsteps, and strategy to the side. Well, that means you lose whatever GIT momentum you had. So you just quit. (I am sure plenty of readers have tried one or more systems designed to replicate success.) You have lost your mojo. You fell off the Get It Together wagon, so you might as well drop the entire thing. You just ate the whole damn cake.

The Happiness Axis

I have a chart that I give to my new leaders. It's similar to the Dunning-Kruger effect.

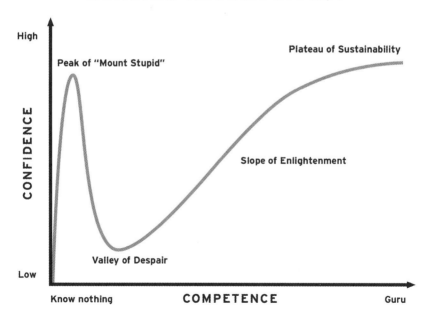

On one axis is happiness. (And don't we all want to be happy and satisfied with our job?) On the other axis is knowledge. That knowledge has to do with your position or promotion—what you need to know to be successful where you are working.

Along the bottom are day zero, day thirty, day sixty, and day ninety. Using the example of a promotion, on day zero when you first become a leader or you get your dream job of VP of sales or you're now a CRO, on the first day, you're so happy—but your knowledge is zero. You feel the energy of having achieved one of your goals. You just know you're on your way! Oh, my naive little buttercup!

As you go through the first thirty days, your happiness slowly declines as your knowledge rises. Why? You discover all the things you don't know. You are overwhelmed.

You start to realize that one of your team members is Debbie Downer. You see a couple of redundant processes that you know can be streamlined. You find out a competitor has a new update—better than the one on the product/service you're trying to sell. You are putting in eighty hours a week to get up to speed. You are exhausted, and you forget the last time you stayed awake more than ten minutes when you put on your favorite Netflix binge-watch. You get the idea.

As your knowledge rises still more at day sixty and then day ninety, your happiness sinks to an all-time low. *This is too much for me. This isn't what I signed up for. I am not sure I am even up to this. I am an* impostor*!*

Basically, at day ninety you hit rock bottom. I actually had a leader who, on day ninety-one, walked into my office and said, "I love working for you, Puja. But I can't do this job anymore."

"Wait, what? You worked so hard to achieve this—to get this leadership role. You worked very hard to get where you are and put in long hours to attain your dream. Now you can't do it?"

She nodded and grabbed a tissue from a box on my desk. (And just so we don't get into gender stereotypes, I've had more than a few men get teary in my office at different points over the years.)

I asked her, "Tell me one more time … how long have you been at this job?" Of course, I already knew the answer.

"Three months, Puja."

"Wow, ninety days, huh. Such a long stretch. You're right, you'll never learn it all. You should quit while you're behind." I said this in the most exaggerated voice and got her mood lifted enough that she gave me a small smile.

I opened my desk drawer, dug into a file, and pulled out the Happiness Axis chart. I pointed. "Here, this is where you are. You are in the pit of despair, the road of never-ending sorrows, the village of heartbreak—or so you think. You have extraordinary knowledge; you've stretched yourself and grown these last three months. But now you are wondering if you have bit off more than you can chew."

"Puja, what am I doing with my life? My team sucks. I suck. Nothing's moving. I'm up against a boulder that I cannot budge."

I stared at her with all sincerity and said, "I'm not letting you quit."

"What do you mean?"

"What do I mean? I'm telling you, you are not quitting. What you are experiencing right now is *normal*. You are going to give me another ninety-day period, end of story."

She looked horrified. "But I'm telling you I can't do this job."

I laughed a little. "Right, because I am in the habit of promoting people who can't do the job. That's what I am all about. I don't give them any of the tools they need. I don't train them. I just love to watch them fail. Let me pop some popcorn. This is better than reality TV."

By now she was half smirking.

I reassured her, "You *can* do this job. You're just at the normal phase of the first ninety days at rock bottom. It feels like you are flailing, drowning … and failing. But you're not."

Don't Forget the Basics

For my leader, overwhelmed, she lost sight of the things she knew, how to get it together. This is why a mentor or accountability partner is so important. When you are wrestling the failure monster, you can forget you actually have some powerful weapons.

I leaned across my desk and smiled. "Let's talk about two or three things that we *can* focus on. Let's drill this down and talk about the first three things that we need to do."

She nodded. (Bonus hint: when confronted with any problem, be open to solutions.)

I asked her, "What's your number one problem?"

"My people."

Now over the years, I have learned that typically, on a team, it's a leader problem or a people problem. I didn't think it was a leader problem. So I asked her who her bottom three performers were. To her credit, she immediately knew who they were and some of their issues.

The next obvious question was if they were on a performance plan. A plan is *not* a punishment. A plan spells out expectations. It clarifies the team's big goals—and then that is reflected in the individual goals of the personal performance plan.

We started there. I could see right away that there were problems. I told her I would help her write the performance plan. That is another advantage of having a mentor. She didn't enter into her leadership position already knowing how to draft these plans and how to monitor them—and how to guide her salespeople. Together we focused the lens on the basics.

1. Activity

2. Hitting the team's numbers

3. Growing the funnel

One, two, three—the basics, just like the alphabet and counting to ten.

So we ticked one item off the list. We identified one problem (or failure, if you will) and set up a plan to turn it around.

Next was another basic. "Who are your top twenty billing customers?"

She rattled them off—again, very informed (as I would have expected).

"Great, have you met with any of them? It's been ninety days."

"Puja, I've been so busy trying to get up to speed on everything I haven't been able to do much else."

"Yes, but if you don't hit your numbers, where are you?" Obviously, contacting these people was the next action step. But it needed to be specific. I wanted to give her a spelled-out goal, a clear direction.

"Next week I want you to come back to discuss your progress and how you are feeling, and I want you to have meetings set with five of those top twenty-five. They can be a month out. But I want those meetings set. The way you position that when you call them is, 'I'm a new leader on the team. I haven't had the opportunity to get to know you yet. You're an extraordinarily important customer for us. I would love to spend thirty minutes with you doing introductions and understanding a little bit more about why you bought our product.'"

She agreed that was a reasonable expectation and approach. We were rolling! Wonderful—two challenges down, one to go (keeping our basics to three).

Next, she felt her team was not doing what she told them to do. That sounded an awful lot to me like a trust issue. My team *trusts* me, and so I never have that problem. And that trust goes both ways.

My suggestions there were gentle. "Make it fun on *Dialing for Dollars* days. Gamify it." I offered her a couple of suggestions.

But it was more than that. Sometimes we *fail* at the simple things. We get so wrapped up in the numbers, the competition, the Excel spreadsheets, and the tech that we don't bring it down to the most important thing—the *people*.

"Why don't you bring them breakfast in the morning and sit with them on the floor as they are doing their sales calls? That way you can coach them immediately."

"I can do that."

"Here's the thing: it's not just about the coaching. They will see you caring, see you wanting to be there with your *team*. You'll be building those relationships."

She nodded. Three things, the basics.

"Come back to me in a week. Focus on those three things."

"I will. But I still want to quit this job."

I just smiled and nodded.

A week later things were improved enough that she was willing to give me ninety days. In that time she weeded out the people unwilling to step up their game. She hired three new people whom she was incredibly excited about. Her team started showing real progress. By the end of forty-five days, she had met with fifteen of her top twenty-five customers and had some new business too. The funnel was taking care of itself by accomplishing these basics.

After the meetings she set up with various customers, she understood those clients better. She knew why they bought our product, and she found a rapport with them. This was also building her confidence.

Of course, after ninety days she didn't quit. She ended up being a leader forever—still in leadership, only now she's a vice president of sales. Sometimes in the face of failure, it's time to revisit the basics.

Time Your Pity Party

My next nonnegotiable success principle is to time your pity party. I'm sure you're wondering what that means. Well, here's the thing. Too many success principle books make it sound as if you have to be "on, on, on" all the time, that you should just bounce back from every unfortunate circumstance. That is simply not human. That's a Stepford-wife kind of cheeriness.

It's OK to feel sorry for yourself, to be bitterly disappointed, to be crushed. Shit happens to each and every one of us. Glossing over your pain will not help you. Gloss over your pain and pretend it's not there for too long, over too many difficult things, and you will find yourself sick physically, mentally, or both.

What I choose to do and coach my people to do is go ahead and throw a pity party. Heck, send out an engraved invitation delivered by carrier pigeon if you want. But you have a time limit. For a small disappointment (anything from not landing an account you were trying for to learning you can't go on the vacation you planned because your partner can't take the week you want off), you might give it an hour. A big disappointment? Let's say you don't land the leadership role you were promised, something you worked toward for months. Take the weekend. But come back on Monday ready to go at it again.

What does your pity party look like? That's as varied as people. For a friend of mine, it means staying in bed and watching zombie movies; for someone else it might be literally crying and letting it all out. Another person might eat a pint of Ben & Jerry's. As long as you are not harming yourself, wallow in it.

Just set a timer. When the alarm goes off, it's time to picture yourself shaking it off, leaving it behind. Learn from it and regroup.

Impostor Syndrome

I mentioned impostor syndrome earlier in the chapter. In the 1970s two psychologists coined the term. It's an extreme self-doubt; a false belief that you are incompetent, lack skills, or cannot compete with others; and a terror of being revealed as a fraud. (Hint: That's a pretty similar thing to fear of failure.) Impostor syndrome can be debilitating. It can cause anxiety, panic attacks, depression, and additional stress.

I know people who don't have MBAs, for example, who panic that they cannot compete in the workplace at the level they aspire to without one. Guess what? Only about 37 percent of North American CEOs have an MBA.[19] (That figure moves to about half of CEOs at Fortune 100 companies.[20]) People feel like impostors about their families (people who want everything to look perfect from the outside), about their talents. They may think they got a promotion or sale because of "luck" and not give themselves any credit. Extreme perfectionism is another symptom.

If you have impostor syndrome, what can you do to combat it?

---

19 "Do I Need an MBA to Be a CEO?" Best Colleges, March 16, 2023, https://www. bestcolleges.com/business/mba/do-i-need-an-mba-to-be-a-ceo/.

20 Ibid.

- Let go of your perfectionistic ways. No one is perfect. You may think if you do everything right, then you'll finally be ready to achieve your dreams. Hate to break it to you. You'll never be able to do everything perfectly.

- Face the facts. Part of impostor syndrome is the things we tell ourselves—which very often are not rooted in truth. The way to combat that is with facts. So if impostor syndrome is telling you that you are failing at your funnel, then it's time to take out your customer relationship management (CRM) data and look at the cold, hard facts. Is it actually true? Or is it just you thinking it's a mess?

- "Fake it till you make it" isn't always the wisest path. Yes, every single person reading this book has had to fake it at some point. Now sometimes it could be as silly an example as when you are in high school, and you haven't read the next chapter of *To Kill a Mockingbird*. So you listen to everyone else in the class's answers, hoping you don't get called on—and if you do, you say stuff that sounds as if you know what you are talking about. We've all been in a work meeting and realized we aren't as prepared as we thought. However, I am talking about being so afraid of people finding out you don't know everything that you never ask for help—and never reveal that you aren't sure of an answer.

- Know that starting something new is a prime time for these feelings and be prepared for them—and don't give them so much weight.

- It's OK to remind yourself how great you are. By that I mean that too many of us will stay in the shadows, telling ourselves we suck. But when something good happens, we don't celebrate it. Yin and yang. You cannot only listen to the bad. And if you were raised to believe modesty and humility are important but heard that lesson a little too much and took it too much to heart, it is perfectly OK to tell yourself, "Good job!" It doesn't mean your ego has grown so large that your head can't fit through the door.

Mental Healthcare

When I sat down to write this book, I promised myself I would talk about mental health. One of the things I've learned as someone who has been so open on the *Huffington Post* and elsewhere about my struggle with fibromyalgia is that I am not alone. Too many of us suffer in silence.

That silence is particularly toxic when it comes to mental health. Thank goodness the stigma about reaching out for mental healthcare and support and therapy has been fading. I consider that one of the silver linings of the COVID-19 pandemic. You could not click through the cable news channels or read a prominent publication like the *New York Times*, the *Guardian*, or pretty much any mainstream news source or magazine without an article or essay on the mental toll the isolation, fear, and uncertainty took on our nation and the world.

Despite the pandemic easing some, the demand for mental health services has never been higher, according to large-scale surveys of psychologists.[21] People are now realizing—and talking about—their mental well-being. We are realizing our quality of life is affected by

---

21   Cara Murez, "Psychologists Overwhelmed by High Demand for Mental Health Care," UPI, November 16, 2022, https://www.upi.com/Health_News/2022/11/16/psychologists-overwhelmed-mental-healthcare/1161668608490/.

physical illness—but the long-term toll of mental health issues is equally debilitating.

One thing I absolutely want to address is women and mental health. As someone with many years of corporate leadership under my belt, I have watched countless women struggle with the concept of "having it all." Sure, you can have it all if you have good childcare, have help at home, and don't expect that you can cook perfectly healthy *and* delicious meals every single night (particularly if you have kids to pick up from school or aftercare, set up with homework, and so on).

"Having it all" has become a hopeless cliché. What does it even mean? Most of the time, especially in the case of women, we often hear we *can't* have it all. And that's true. No one can spin every plate—much as some of us type As try. Having it all means *not* having all the work be your responsibility in your partnership. Or it means delegating childcare, domestic help, and personal assistance tasks. Doing this in a strategic way is foundational to your mental health and your success at work.

Long before the pandemic ushered in hybrid work and work-from-home scenarios, I trusted my people to get their work done as they needed, as long as they did it. Do I care if you come in at seven one morning to clear a bunch of stuff off your desk so you can leave at two to go to the dentist? I have always reassured my people that I "see" them. I encourage women to not rush back to the office after a pregnancy if they don't have to. My god, you created a *human being*. Six weeks is not enough; I have spearheaded changing maternity and paternity leave at various companies where I worked.

In addition, our mental health worsens when we compare ourselves with others. Curated Instagram feeds, for instance, are a real culprit. Let me ask you a question—and be honest. When was the last time you took a *horrible* picture and posted it? You don't put your unedited life out there, so don't think other people are. Most of us are guilty of using filters and retaking selfies. We try to make our lives look so easy—and meanwhile we're pulling our hair out from stress.

We all need to get a lot more honest. When we reveal our actual truth, when we are vulnerable, we're actually helping the world in a positive way by showing others that we all have a hard time, or we need a helping hand from time to time. We are working ourselves to death sometimes and comparing ourself with others, and one of the things that suffers is our mental well-being.

YOUR COPING SKILLS AND HABITS

A subset of mental health is your coping skills. This may seem obvious, but I have to say it. If the way you unwind every night is drinking a bottle of wine, screaming at your kids, sleeping too much, overeating junk, or running up your credit card with online shopping, you need to find new ways to deal with "pain" because that's what it's about. We don't hide under the covers and sleep away the entire weekend if we're coping with our workload in a healthy way.

We're going to tackle this issue in our Straight Talk section, but let's just name a few positive coping habits:

- Meditation

- Moderate amounts of exercise

- Deep breathing

- Journaling

- Hobbies that bring you joy (painting, gardening, listening to—or creating—music)

And don't forget perhaps the greatest tool of all: talking. Whether that's talking to a therapist, your best friend or partner, a trusted work confidant or mentor, or whoever it is, sharing your struggles is essential.

Rebounding and Failure

Time to be honest here. I just advised you to talk about your struggles, so I will share one of mine.

When I attained a major leadership position, I knew I was struggling. My "happiness index" was just as I explained it earlier. I was learning my way but at the expense of happiness. I was trying to drive revenue, but I didn't have the data I needed. (And by now after our earlier "Winning Formula" chapter, you know I *love* data.) I also was having to make some tough calls that I needed to (or thought I did). I could "feel" the energy in the room toward me from both the board and my people.

After thirty days or so, I confided in my husband that I was certain everyone hated me, and on top of it, I was having to learn a massive amount of tech—and my brain hurt from it all. Oh, and my assistant was brand new. I was trying to onboard her when I still wasn't done with all my own onboarding. It was a cluster-you-know-what.

Well, my husband is an extremely wise man. He also knows me *so* well. And he told me, "Puja, don't you coach people on how to deal with all this? What's the most important thing to focus on?" Don't you hate when your partner is right?

I tackled two things—the data first. I figured out what I needed and how to get it. So I had someone working on that as a special project. My second issue was having to let someone go. For reasons I cannot get into because of confidentiality, of course, my VP of sales was hopelessly mismatched for his position. (I honestly think he was relieved when we parted ways because I think he was miserable in the job.) I was then able to hire someone I thought was ideal and was going to bring a needed energy.

But there was one last "important" thing, number three. My team hated me. Bear can be pretty straightforward. He said, "Puja, not only are you going to need to spend more time with them but you're also going to have to ask for feedback from them, honest feedback." It's because feedback goes both ways. "You're going to have to listen, Puja, and eat it if you have to." Don't you *really* hate it when your partner is right?

I went in there, and I asked them to let me have it. And they did. Basically their bottom line was, "You haven't spent enough time understanding us. You're trying to make things very operational when we don't even have the basics. You're not listening to us. You're not allowing us to give you solid feedback before you're jumping ten steps ahead."

Blah, blah, not good blah! It was one of the worst days I've ever had in my leadership career. I timed my pity party—and let me tell you, it lasted a whole weekend. But the minute that party was over, I kicked the pity to the curb. (No, it cannot be like your drunk uncle who overstays every party by falling asleep on the couch.)

I knew that once the party was over, it was time to face things head-on—and take action because the *one* thing that will doom you to continued failure is remaining stuck, doing nothing. Obviously something was broken. Now you have to fix it or clean it up. Imagine you have a beautiful vase on a table in your foyer. Someone knocks it over on the tiled floor, and it shatters into a million pieces. You don't leave the shards on the ground to cut yourself—over and over again. You sweep up the mess.

Now here's the happy ending. I *listened*. (Another tip: if you want to learn from failure, you have to listen, and you have to look inward and really analyze what went wrong.) That team ended up being tight knit and positive (and successful). When I was away from the office for a stretch, a couple of them called me and told me they missed me! (And I missed them.)

STRAIGHT TALK
FROM PUJA

All right, failure sucks. But you have to take away its power. Does failure feel like the *monster* under the bed, or have you shone a big flashlight under there and realized it's just a setback for now?

Here are three exercises I want you to do. I'll wait. Go get a pen.

1. The first is your happiness index.

HAPPINESS INDEX

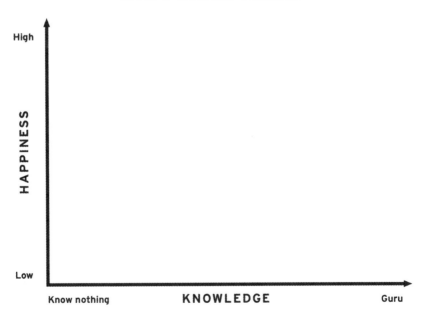

Where are you on the chart? Is your happiness low and your knowledge high? The opposite? Or have you found a middle ground? If your happiness isn't where you want it, I'd like you to "give me" thirty days of *really* working the principles in this book to see if you can't nudge that index a little higher by regrouping, learning new coping skills, or shutting up the impostor voice in your head.

2. Be honest. (And your mom was right. If you aren't honest about things, you're only hurting yourself.)

What is your top coping skill?

_____

Is it a healthy one?

_____

Do you need to learn a new one?

_____

What can you be doing in your life to give yourself and your mental health a break? A Think Day? Sharing with someone—a friend, a therapist, a mentor—how you are feeling in times of stress?

_____

3. Be honest.

When was the last time you failed at something that was important to you?

_____

Have you rebounded?

_____

Why or why not?

_____

What can you do differently now that you are getting it together?

_____

Guess what? We're at the last chapter. Time to put it all together— and finish with a pep talk.

Now That You've Got It Together, Get Ready for Big Results

One can choose to go back toward
safety or forward toward growth.

—ABRAHAM MASLOW

Do you feel like you are starting to get it together? Are you focusing on your three goals for the current quarter? Do not tell me you didn't write them down. Go back to the beginning of the book and start again—do not pass Go; do not collect $200. If you've written them down, bravo. Are you swiping left on anything that does not get you to your goals? Are you figuring out the breaks in your machine—and how to fix them?

I knew I wanted my last chapter to remind you what it looks like to *not* have it together and what it looks like when you implement all the exercises, mindset, and new tools in this book.

The Sort-of Mess

When I made it to the C-suite, it was the culmination of ambition instilled in me from childhood by my hardworking parents. From the first time my mother set a timer for me to practice piano, she was making sure I knew that hard work is the pathway to success. You are not going to sit down at the piano after a month of lessons and play Rachmaninoff.

From the first time I followed my father through his workplace and saw how he encouraged and cared about his employees, I was learning how to treat people as the real treasure and value of a company. He was modeling empathy and compassion—while still wanting to draw the best from the people he was leading.

Over the years I've watched peers and colleagues succeed. And I have watched them fail and have to try something new. I've watched people soar. And I've watched people get stuck or plateau. And I learned a few things.

Plenty of people look like they sort of have it together. They are sort of successful and a sort-of mess. The sort-of people, I have nearly always found, are not lacking in intelligence. Some have been very intellectually smart. The sort-of people aren't lacking in ambition. They want some of the same things I want or you want.

What the sort-of people do not have, though, is discipline and the will and determination to get it together. They will get halfway there. But then it starts to get tough. The air of the C-suite is rarified because it's, well, very hard to get there, and it's the rare people who will do what it takes.

Every single ambitious person comes to a crossroads. This is true no matter the field, no matter the career. It is true of baseball players who want to get to the majors, of musicians who want to cut an EP, of the reporter who wants to make it to editor in chief, or the daughter of immigrants who wants to make it to the C-suite. Every single person who wants the big dream reaches the crossroads where *natural talent is not enough.*

To get to the next level in anything ambitious requires the hard sacrifices—the long hours going for an MBA or a certification of some sort, swiping left on too many social obligations, rising early to write that novel for an hour before the day job. It's rising when it's still dark out to go running and then lift weights. Whatever it is, you have to decide whether to go for it, to cut out all the distractions and noise. You decide whether you're going to do as Abraham Maslow, the world-famous psychologist, said. You will either grow or play it safe.

You can keep doing what the sort-ofs are doing and "hope" that you get some lucky breaks. I "hope" you have the *clarity* to know that sort of applying these principles will get you sort-of-good results.

The Monday Morning Huddle

I'm the boss you need, the coach you need. And we're about to have our huddle. I do this every Monday with my team. I choose Monday because that's the way to set our week into motion.

Here's the first thing to know in the huddle: the Get It Together mindset always works.

"Puja, come on. You've told us in the book you've had to fire sales leaders ill suited to their job. People miss their numbers all the time. It doesn't always work."

It does.

I've failed. I've been laid off. I've had to take two steps back to eventually go four steps forward. I've been absolutely rock bottom. My teams have been rock bottom. (Remember, I once inherited a team I called the Bad News Bears.) So what? The game is only over when you're dead. If you're not dead and are reading this, get back up and dust yourself off.

When I get in there with my team and we are not landing the numbers we want, let me tell you, I pace back and forth on my three-inch heels, and I'm that coach at halftime who has to kick some proverbial ass and get everyone fired up. I often start with the hard questions: What's the weak link? What's your sort-of? Did you do what you were supposed to do yesterday, last week, last month, or did you cut corners?

Did you do all the exercises in the book? Three goals? (Don't tell me you have ten goals. No—three.) Have you implemented changes and habits for sixty-six days? If you didn't see the results after two weeks and decided to go back to how you've always done things, I need you to stop right there. Two weeks is not going to create the life you want! These principles have to become second nature. If *your* way has not gotten you to where you want to be, what makes you think your methods will work now? It's time to try something new.

"Puja, I was doing good for a month, but now I've fallen off the Get It Together wagon."

Of course you did! Come on! You are doing something new. Learning new skills, a new approach, or a new way of being is difficult—and even courageous. You're going to have setbacks.

Remember our happiness index. We will all spend some time in the pit of despair singing the "I can't believe I thought I could do this" blues.

Of course you can do this! Are you "thinking" about all these great ideas now that you've spent hours reading this book? Stop thinking. *Do it.* Critical thinking is important. *But thinking and thinking without an action plan is just daydreaming.* Stop daydreaming and start making things happen.

What's your tone for the week? Are you fired up? Ready to relentlessly execute? Roar of the Beast mode?

What Are You Avoiding?

I want you to get it together. But that means you're going to have to do the hard things, those things you've been avoiding. I saved this topic for the last chapter because if I put it in the first chapter, you'd be scared. Now you should feel like you have a plan; you have the winning formula. It's not so scary.

We have all watched people stay in relationships that are long past their sell-by date. Maybe you are even in one now. No one thinks divorce is a rollicking good time. I know the thinking sometimes: "I am barely holding it together with another warm body in the house to help me with the kids, the schedules we keep, the household chores," or "I am not sure I can financially do this all on my own." No one wants to have to deal with lawyers with all the ins and outs of tough decisions.

The things we avoid are the things we know about ourselves and our lives that must change in order for us to get it together.

It might not be a relationship. If you haven't woken up completely on fire with passion for your job in a couple of years and you are just going through the motions, it's time to move on! No, I don't think anyone is thrilled with the idea of updating their résumé and reaching out to contacts on LinkedIn, but being a zombie at the office isn't fun either.

Cold calls—oh my god, do we all hate them. But faking the numbers and telling your boss you made twenty calls when you didn't isn't going to get you what you want.

We never talk about what we're avoiding. Why? Because we are ashamed. The things we avoid are the things we know about ourselves and our lives that must change in order for us to get it together and attain the life and career we want. We know it. Deep down we really do.

Most of us are not blind to our weaknesses. Think of the person with the terrible temper at work who *knows* they blow their stack and that it is not helping their team—but they are not even going to *look* at why they lose it in that way or how to change that. "It's just the way I am" is an excuse that's not going to cut it anymore. Think of #MeToo. A whole culture at work where people said or did inappropriate things was tolerated for generations. That may have been how it was—but it is not how it is now. If you have a problem with your behavior, not changing it is laziness or willful disregard for the people around you.

Your Someday Is Now

I have a story—a kind of crazy story, but I love it. You see, my husband and I bought a beautiful house in Miami when we moved here. We did some extensive remodeling, and one of the things we did was redo the bathrooms. I picked out a vanity, mirrors, sconces, and a toilet, not just *any* toilet but the Rolls-Royce of toilets—only I really did not quite think it through.

You see, this toilet was so special, with settings and water-saving features. I don't know why I picked out this supersonic toilet because, face it, this is not something we buy every day. However, what I did not know was that, in all Miami, there was *one* guy who installed, repaired, and knew all about this luxury item.

Well, we needed repairs on ours. My husband will talk to anyone and everyone, and so this *one* guy came to repair it. They got to talking, and I was overhearing this whole conversation from my office. This particular plumber was so in demand among luxury home buyers that he could have back-to-back appointments for the next three years. Contractors used him; homeowners used him. (I promise, this toilet story is going someplace.)

This plumber was making a crazy amount of money! And as he was talking with Bear, he said, "I ran into some of my high school friends at a bar, and they were talking about the same nonsense [he used a few expletives, so you can imagine those] they were doing last year and the year before and the year before and the year before that." Heck, Bruce Springsteen wrote a whole song about people who relive the "best" times of their lives in the past, the "glory days."

Mr. Fixer continued, "They're just not willing to put in the work. Look, do you think I liked fixing these supersonic toilets at first? No. I had to learn. I had to get certified. I had to challenge myself, but now I'm the only one in Miami Beach who knows how to do these repairs, so I'm in constant high demand, and the money's never going to stop flowing."

Look, we all can be those high school friends, imagining a someday. And so I saved this for the last part of the book because I didn't want to scare you. This book encourages deep change. And when you truly decide to get it together, it's possible you will lose 95 percent of the people around you. It makes people uncomfortable when someone else reminds them that they are stuck.

You have to know that it's OK to swipe left on those friends who aren't on the same path. People who make deep-seated changes like this experience upheaval. But you're not the first, and you most certainly will not be the last. To make deep-seated change like this, there is sacrifice involved. And sacrifice means that you may not have things in common anymore with the sort-of people.

I don't think there's any successful person who has not had to shed some people who were deadweight on them.

The fact is I don't think there's any successful person who has not had to shed some people who were deadweight on them, who were not supporting them in their goals. When you get it together, you move into a different space. You begin attracting the positive and getting rid of the negative. When you flip a switch and you're in that growth mindset all the time, some people will fall away.

Maybe you feel like you would be a bad person if you "outgrew" some of your crew. Maybe you feel like you need permission to change so much. If that's what you need, well, here you go.

Permission Granted

I give you permission to do this program and embrace these principles. I want the best for you, and I think you know deep down inside what it's going to take to achieve your goals. Everything to this point has been learning and practicing for greatness. Like the timer with the piano, you have been waiting for this. The practice is done. Recital time is here.

I give you permission to swipe left. You need to in order to shut out distractions and focus.

I give you permission to say the word *no*—often.

I give you permission to get off the hamster wheel and make forward progress, not spin in place.

I give you permission to work hard, really hard. That may make some people uncomfortable. That's OK. If you are making people uncomfortable, you're doing something right.

I give you permission to be ambitious. You must be ethical—but there is no sin in wanting to pursue big dreams. "Reach" dreams. It's OK to say those things out loud too. Having ambition doesn't mean you think you're better than anyone else. It means you are focused on where you want to go.

I give you permission to try hard things and fail. That's how you will learn. So it's a lesson wrapped around a failure, which is kind of like an éclair—and pastry can't be bad.

I give you permission to have the hard conversations. Just because you say the difficult parts out loud does not make you "mean."

I give you permission to be a fighter.

I give you permission to roar like the beast. You're fierce. You got this.

I give you permission to take time to critically think.

I give you permission to take a day to regroup and maybe revise your plan.

I give you permission to apply the winning formula. Define your pillars and go for it.

I give you permission to feel pain and to learn new coping skills and tools to transform pain into triumph.

I give you permission to be more successful than [fill in the blank: your parents, your siblings, your childhood best friend, your neighbor].

I give you permission to have hope, to really want something with all your heart.

I give you permission to have clarity—to take a hard look and an inventory of you and what you have tried before and to try something new this time.

I give you permission to *get it together*.

I decided to end the book not with Straight Talk but with a few words to convey to you what an honor and a privilege it has been to take this journey with you. I wish every single reader nothing but the greatest success—and please, if the Get It Together mindset has changed your life for the better, be sure to reach out to me and tell me your successes. May we change ourselves and then the world together.

ABOUT THE AUTHOR

Puja Bhola Rios is a C-level revenue executive for a Fortune 300 company. Previously Puja spent seven years at Xerox and thirteen years at CareerBuilder as their senior vice president of enterprise sales and customer success. While at CareerBuilder, Puja founded and ran her company's women's alliance, CareerBuildHER. In addition, Puja prides herself on her work as a chronic pain advocate and blogger. She is the author of the *Huffington Post* feature blog *Me vs. Fibromyalgia*, as well as a contributor to Thrive Global and The Mighty. Puja lives in Miami Beach with her husband and their two dogs, JZ and RiRi.